D1546410

# *More business English*

## PARA DUMMIES™

**Revisado por los editores
de Gestión 2000**

Obra editada en colaboración con Centro Libros PAPF, S.L.U. – España

Edición publicada mediante acuerdo con Wiley Publishing, Inc.
© ...For Dummies y los logos de Wiley Publishing, Inc. son marcas registradas
utilizadas bajo licencia exclusiva de Wiley Publishing, Inc.

© 2013, Centro de Libros, PAPF, S.L.U.
Grupo Planeta – Barcelona, España

Reservados todos los derechos

© 2013, Editorial Planeta Mexicana, S.A. de C.V.
Bajo el sello editorial CEAC M.R.
Avenida Presidente Masarik núm. 111, 2o. piso
Colonia Chapultepec Morales
C.P. 11570, México, D. F.
www.editorialplaneta.com.mx

Primera edición impresa en España: enero de 2013
ISBN: 978-84-329-0128-7

Primera edición impresa en México: marzo de 2013
ISBN: 978-607-07-1564-8

Impreso en los talleres de Litográfica Ingramex, S.A. de C.V.
Centeno núm. 162, colonia Granjas Esmeralda, México, D.F.
Impreso en México - *Printed in Mexico*

# Sumario

## Capítulo 4: Atender al cliente y tratar con él ...... 99

# Introducción

* * * * * * * * * * * * * * * * * * * * * * * * * * *

*E*l mundo de los negocios es apasionante. Además de un modo muy interesante de ganarte la vida, te ofrece un amplio abanico de oportunidades y desafíos personales, así como la posibilidad de conocer a mucha gente y, seguramente, también la de viajar a otras ciudades y países. Como ves, te brinda muchas cosas, pero también te exige otras.

Entre esas exigencias está la de hacer bien tu trabajo, como ya pudiste ver en *Business English para Dummies*, y esto supone tener un trato exquisito con los clientes: ofrecerles precios ventajosos para cerrar la venta en condiciones favorables para ambas partes, saber leer sus necesidades para convencerlos de que salen ganando si aceptan tu oferta, conseguir que una toma de decisiones favorable a los clientes sea también beneficiosa para los intereses de la empresa, manejar los departamentos de ventas en tu país y el extranjero, servir un producto óptimo y a salvo de imitaciones, y fijarse objetivos razonables. Tan importante como captar nuevos clientes es recuperarlos y fidelizarlos, aprender de ellos, y muchas cosas más que irás aprendiendo a medida que avances en la lectura de este libro.

Pero además hay un elemento totalmente imprescindible para todo aquel que quiera dedicarse a los negocios: saber inglés y, por lo tanto, conocer y dominar toda la jerga particular del mundo empresarial en esta lengua. Por esa razón el contenido de este libro está escrito íntegramente en inglés.

Así pues, no sólo vas a aprender los mejores consejos y técnicas sobre ventas o sobre el trato con los clientes, sino que además lo harás en el idioma internacional de los negocios, el inglés. Puedes estar seguro de que después de leer este libro (y *Business*

*English para Dummies*) te habrás convertido en un auténtico o una auténtica *business (wo)man*.

# Acerca de este libro

Este libro está dirigido a todas aquellas personas que cumplan los siguientes dos requisitos: primero, querer adentrarse en la "cocina" del mundo de los negocios, conocer detalles sobre técnicas de venta, ganar nuevos clientes o abrir una franquicia en el extranjero, entre otras muchas cuestiones; y segundo, querer aprender todo esto en inglés, la lengua que van a necesitar para aplicar esos conocimientos.

Muchas de las estrategias y las técnicas que encontrarás en estas páginas pueden ayudarte a rendir mejor como miembro de un equipo de ventas o como gestor de una empresa. Lo que te ofrece este libro es una guía práctica para lograr que tu equipo de ventas o tu empresa obtengan buenos resultados, un buen recurso para afrontar ese gran desafío.

El contenido de este libro se ha elaborado a partir de una serie de entrevistas realizadas a distintos directivos, jefes de ventas y otros profesionales de varias empresas internacionales. Este procedimiento garantiza que la información reflejada esté avalada por el conocimiento y la experiencia de estos expertos.

No es éste un manual de capítulos tediosos que tendrás ir leyendo página a página. *More business English para Dummies* es una experiencia distinta e innovadora. Tú marcarás tu ritmo de aprendizaje leyendo cuanto desees y en el orden que quieras. Recuerda que puedes saltar de un capítulo a otro, o de una sección a otra, y detenerte donde más te interese.

# Convenciones usadas en este libro

Con el fin de facilitar la lectura de este libro, se ha establecido la siguiente convención:

✔ Se han marcado con **negrita y cursiva** todas aquellas palabras de difícil comprensión o que pertenecen a la jerga propia del mundo de los negocios. Podrás consultar su significado (descrito también en inglés) al final de cada sección, en el apartado "Palabras para recordar".

Asimismo, y por si hay algún término que no quede del todo claro, al final del libro encontrarás un pequeño vocabulario inglés-español que te ayudará a resolver cualquier duda.

También te hemos incluido un glosario que además de aclararte términos te puede servir para aprender sinónimos y ampliar tu vocabulario.

La puntuación y la ortografía son parte del idioma, y como antes o después hay que escribir, es conveniente prestar atención a esos aspectos y ser consciente de que igual que las palabras cambian entre idiomas, las normas y los usos de la puntuación también lo hacen. Por lo que respecta a la puntuación, el idioma inglés se rige por varias tradiciones, que, en términos generales, pueden encuadrarse en dos escuelas: la estadounidense y la británica. Habida cuenta que el inglés de los negocios irradia, mayoritariamente, desde Estados Unidos, en este libro se sigue esa tradición; los rasgos principales diferentes de la tradición británica son el uso masivo de la coma y la colocación de comas y puntos dentro de las comillas y los paréntesis.

## ¿Quién eres tú?

Para escribir este libro tuvimos que suponer ciertas cosas acerca de ti y sobre lo que podrías esperar de un libro titulado *Business English para Dummies*. Estas son algunas de nuestras hipótesis:

✔ Te dedicas al mundo de los negocios, dominas el inglés, y quieres reforzar o ampliar tus conocimientos a partir de la experiencia de los grandes profesionales que nos han ayudado a realizar este libro.

✔ Te dedicas al mundo de los negocios de ámbito internacional y, aunque reforzar tus conocimientos nunca viene mal, lo que deseas sobre todo es potenciar tu nivel de inglés orientado al mundo empresarial.

✔ Aunque dominas el inglés, sabes muy poco sobre negocios. A pesar de eso, te encantaría adentrarte en ese mundo aprendiendo algunos de sus secretos y trucos.

✔ Conoces el título *Coaching para Dummies* y despertó tu curiosidad.

Si te ves reflejado en alguna de estas situaciones, no hay duda: ¡has encontrado el libro perfecto!

# Iconos usados en este libro

A lo largo del libro verás unos pequeños iconos en los márgenes. Con ellos pretendemos llamar tu atención de manera especial. Los ponemos en inglés para que te familiarices con el idioma. Significan lo siguiente:

Este icono destaca ideas prácticas y consejos que pueden ayudarte en el mundo de los negocios.

Este icono sirve como recordatorio para que no olvides información importante.

Usamos este icono para alertarte sobre posibles peligros o escollos y para advertirte sobre errores que debes evitar.

Este icono destaca el resultado de la aplicación de la estrategia o de la política empresarial que se esté explicando en ese momento.

# ¿Y ahora qué?

No tienes por qué leer este libro de principio a fin; léelo a tu gusto. Puedes empezar por el capítulo 1 e ir avanzando o, si lo prefieres, puedes echarle una ojeada al sumario y sumergirte directamente en aquellos capítulos o apartados que más te interesen.

# Capítulo 1

# Reuniones y negociaciones

*U*no de los aspectos fundamentales de toda reunión de negocios, capaz de paralizar acuerdos ventajosos para ambas partes, es la fijación del precio del servicio. Hay que evitar malentendidos idiomáticos al abordar esta cuestión, ya que del buen entendimiento entre las partes puede depender el que se cierre o no una venta. Por todo ello hay que saber transmitirle al cliente en qué consiste la política de precios de la empresa, así como los beneficios que éste puede obtener aunque pague por el producto más de lo que había pensado.

Un buen vendedor tiene que saber transmitir en qué estriba el valor añadido de su producto (ya sea éste emocional, material o de resultado), así como marcar los tiempos de la negociación para acelerarla en el momento adecuado y, de este modo, evitar contratiempos.

Con todo esto aprenderás a valorar tu tiempo y el de tu cliente. ¡Buena venta, pues!

# *Do* not be afraid of *price negotiations*

Negotiating the price is part of the daily business for salespeople. That is why it is ***imperative*** that salespeople always prepare well for price discussions and do ***not lapse into*** a monotonous routine.

Many salespeople are uncomfortable discussing prices. They are afraid of losing a deal and ***reluctantly*** give rebates ***when in doubt***, although it might not have been necessary. This can be avoided if sales representatives make clear to themselves the most important principles for discussing and negotiating prices:

✔ In most of the cases, the price plays an essential role but is certainly not the ***sole*** criterion on which the customer bases his decision.

✔ Even a ***steep*** price may not be a disadvantage, especially when it is "sold" ***accordingly*** to the customer. For it is undoubtedly clear that ***superb*** quality has its price – cheap products would, if anything, ***make the customer suspicious***.

✔ Also a ***decisive*** factor is the motivation that ***prompts*** a customer ***to desire*** a ***particular*** product: If it ***aids*** him in an emergency of some sort because, for example, he needs a solution practically "over night," the benefit he ***derives from*** the product will ***outweigh*** the price.

✔ Customers are more likely to demand a rebate after they have already decided to purchase a product. Especially when the customer has a very particular conception of the product and ***is agreeable towards*** the offer in every detail, this ***indicates*** that he is ready to purchase ***regardless***.

✔ Since customers usually set a price limit for themselves and keep it visually present in their minds, salespeople should do the same and concretely determine how far they can go. It should be the uppermost goal to **adhere to** the original price, however.

✔ The more transparent the price is, the less **leeway** the customer has for **levelling it down**. That is why it makes sense **to elucidate** the components which make up the price, for example, expenses for research and development, production/manufacturing, material, machinery, labour time (particularly for specialists) and so forth.

✔ The customer himself needs good arguments for "selling" a high-priced product to his company or rather for selling it to his own customers. Therefore, many customers **appreciate it greatly** if the sales representative prepares them for this situation and accompanies and supports them during their own presentation.

## Communicate the price properly

Salespeople also have to be able to "sell" a product's price with their personality, their **demeanour**, and their body language. Some important rules:

✔ Stick by your products' pricing. If you start being **apologetic** ("I haven't made up these prices"), it will **ring hollow**. The customer realises that the salesperson does not completely stand behind the product he is selling. This will make it easy **to corner him**.

✔ Do not regard discussions about price or requests for rebates as something unpleasant. Instead, consider it as something entirely normal that is simply part of your trade. Make it an objective to feel completely at ease when discussing prices with customers.

✔ Make yourself realise that a self-assured and steadfast salesperson, who does not let himself be unsettled or **cajoled into** something, will impress his customers. You win respect when you stay polite and friendly, yet *remain unresponsive to* excessive demands.

✔ Never let yourself be *coerced* into a confrontation, always remain friendly. Even if you are annoyed with a customer, try to give a *disarming smile*. This will automatically make you come across as more comfortable, relaxed, and competent. You can gain time by first responding to a customer demand with a smile.

✔ *Sink deep into your memory* never ever to make a concession on a price rebate straight away. Allow yourself a pause to think. If your pause takes too long, some customers may start to feel uneasy and realise that their demand was excessive. Pauses like these are often more effective than immediately saying "no."

---

## Palabras para recordar

**to not be afraid of something:** to not be fearful of or nervous about something

**imperative:** very important, crucial, necessary, indispensable, vital

**to not lapse into:** to not slide, slip, submerge, or drift into

**reluctantly:** unwillingly, half-heartedly, grudgingly, unenthusiastically

**when in doubt:** when undecided, uncertain, unsure, or doubtful

**sole:** only, single, one and only, solitary

**steep:** high, expensive, costly

**accordingly:** appropriately, correspondingly, properly, suitably

**superb:** excellent, first-rate, first-class

**to make someone suspicious:** to cause someone to become doubtful, unsure, sceptical, wary, or leery

*(continúa)*

### *Continuación*

**decisive:** deciding, determining, critical

**to prompt:** to cause, to induce, to incite, to impel,
to encourage, to provoke

**to desire:** to want, to wish for, to long for, to set one's heart on

**particular:** specific, individual

**to aid:** to help, to support, to serve

**to derive from:** to get, receive, acquire, obtain, or gain from

**to outweigh:** to be more important than, to take
precedence over

**to be agreeable towards:** to consent to, to accept,
to approve of, to assent to

**to indicate:** to be a sign, to signify, to show, to reveal,
to imply

**regardless:** at any rate, in any case, anyhow,
no matter what

**to adhere to:** to stick to, to stay with, to remain with, to not
swerve from

**leeway:** room to manoeuvre, room to operate, elbowroom,
freedom, flexibility

**to level the price down:** to beat down, knock down,
or cut the cost

**to elucidate:** to explain, to make clear, to clarify, to reveal

**to appreciate something greatly:** to be very thankful
or grateful for something

**demeanour:** manner, conduct, behaviour

**apologetic:** remorseful, contrite, regretful

**to ring hollow:** to not seem credible, authentic, genuine,
or convincing

**to corner someone:** to trap someone, to pin someone
down, to back someone into a corner

*(continúa)*

---

### Continuación

**to be cajoled into something:** to be wheedled or coaxed into something

---

**to remain unresponsive to something:** to stay indifferent or impassive to something

---

**to coerce:** to force, to pressure, to bully

---

**disarming smile:** charming, persuasive, or winning beam

---

**to sink deep into one's memory:** to learn by heart, to commit to one's memory

---

# Benefit beats price

Sales people, who focus their presentation strictly on customer benefit, don't need *to fear* price objections Alfred A., a sales representative for an outside supplier from Essen, had no explanation for a phenomenon he was experiencing, *"I noticed that customers started coming up with price objections just as I was giving a detailed explanation of the product advantages."* But as soon as a customer told him openly, *"**That may all be fine and dandy**, but **what do I get out of it?**,"* the *truth dawned on him*. *"I realised that I had **disregarded**, one **crucial** step: to explain to the customer how he can benefit from the product."*

This experience *prompted* the sales representative *to reassess* his sales argument, *"Now **I'm no longer content** just knowing what the product can do but I think about how it can benefit the customer."* Alfred A. *encountered* a basic problem that his colleagues were also confronted with, *"When we were introduced to the latest products, we always received a lot of information from our company, which, for the most part, **consisted of** technical **papers** and data sheets. Even we had difficulty in **figuring them out**."*

## *In-house workshops*

Alfred A. and his colleagues **approached** their sales manager about this problem. *"We made it clear that we are much too fixated on the product features which really* **puts customers off**" reports the sales representative. *"Then we sat down together in workshops and figured out what to improve and how to go about it."*

Alfred A. is very pleased with the results, *"We* **were determined** *to get to the bottom of the matter: What do our customers want? Where do they have problems? What is it that will benefit them?"*

During the workshop it became clear to the sales representatives that often the most **obvious** things are important to the customer and that there is much he's just not interested in, *"If I read all the technical data to the customer, he'll forget them quickly. But if I tell him that this product* **is suited for** *a number of* **purposes** *and that it saves him time and costs – then the customer really knows what benefit he gets if he buys."*

## Palabras para recordar

**to fear:** to worry about, to dread, to be afraid of

**that may all be fine and dandy:** that may be quite alright, satisfactory, or acceptable

**what do I get out of it:** how do I profit or benefit from it

**the truth dawned on him:** reality struck or occurred to him

**to disregard:** to ignore, to forget about, to overlook, to turn a blind eye to

**crucial:** important, essential, decisive, key

**to prompt:** to induce, to motivate, to cause, to encourage

**to reassess:** to re-examine, to re-evaluate, to reconsider, to have another look at

**to no longer be content:** to not be satisfied or comfortable any longer

*(continúa)*

## *Emphasise* the customer benefit

According to Dr. Irene Glockner-Holme, a sales expert from Stadtbergen, *"It's easy to walk into the 'benefit **trap**' and talk about the product advantages instead of the benefit it provides to the customer."* She explains that a product is not beneficial *per se*. Only if the product **is applied** correctly, the customer **derives** an advantage from it. This advantage is the customer benefit and it should be emphasised clearly. Here are some examples:

✔ The product benefit of an innovative measuring **device** for production lies in even more precise measuring. The customer benefit, however, lies in the decrease of the production costs.

✔ The product benefit of a navigation system lies in being guided automatically to your destination. The customer benefit lies in arriving relaxed and safe at your destination.

✔ The product benefit of automatic machine **maintenance** lies in not having to take care of anything. The customer benefit lies in, for example, increased safety and time **gained**.

---

### *Continuación*

**to encounter:** to come across or upon

**to consist of:** to be made up of, to contain, to include, to comprise

**paper:** treatise, study, report, analysis

**to figure something out:** to understand or comprehend something

**to approach:** to come up to, to talk to, to speak to

**to put someone off:** to discourage, dissuade, dishearten, or repel someone

**to be determined:** to be resolved, set, or intent

**obvious:** apparent, visible, noticeable

*(continúa)*

## *Continuación*

**to be suited for something:** to be appropriate, apt, or fitting for something

**purpose:** use, function, task

**to emphasise:** to call attention to, to highlight, to accentuate, to underline

**trap:** snare, net, deception

**to be applied:** to be used, employed, utilised, or operated

**to derive:** to get, to gain, to obtain

**device:** tool, utensil, instrument

**maintenance:** servicing, overhaul, check

**to gain:** to win, to acquire, to obtain, to build up

# *The magic word is value*

Always ***mention*** the value. Only talk about the price if you really have to. Always focus your presentation on the value of your product or service. ***Keep in mind*** that the ***perceived*** value may be completely different from one customer to the next.

The following examples serve ***to make you aware of*** a product's ***varied*** values and to have the ***appropriate*** argumentation ready when you need it.

## *Emotional value*

Even though emotional value is subjective, it does play a ***vital*** role in the buying decision.

Emotional value may ***consist of***:

✔ owning something that not everyone has or ***is able to afford***

> ✔ *rewarding oneself for something*
> ✔ giving *recognition* to oneself
> ✔ *taking a liking to something*
> ✔ *expressing* one's individuality and personality.

In this *instance*, the added value lies, above all, in a personal, subjective *gain*. Positive self-image, prestige, recognition, and greater *self-esteem* are also part of this gain.

## Material value

In some cases, material value can be *substantiated by* numbers. For example, a *slight* decrease in value or a high *resale value* of machines or *durable consumer goods* can be documented. *Preservation of value* because of a product's *low tendency to break down* or very little *wear and tear* is also considered a material (added) value.

Some products may even provide an increase in value. These may be, for example, *rare*, limited products with *collector's value* that may *fetch* high prices.

Just the same, the material preservation of value may be the result of a measure or investment, for example, the *refurbishing* of a building.

## Resulting value

Added value *may* also *be created* by the product's use. Production and product quality, for instance, can be greatly improved by using a modern machine. In this way the products, manufactured by the customer company, increase in value.

The following points may also *constitute* added value:

> ✔ quicker and more efficient manufacturing
> ✔ cost savings, for example, personnel costs

✔ increase in delivery speed

✔ reduction of **storage costs** because of just-in time delivery

## Asking specific questions

By using a specific questioning technique, you may **induce customers to** come up with their own arguments **in favour of** making a purchase. At the same time, you'll be able to find out what the customer thinks is the greatest added value of a product or service.

 Following are some examples of questions you could ask:

✔ What **bothers** you most with…?

✔ What has kept you, so far, from searching for a solution for…?

✔ Why do you prefer to work with… **rather than with**…?

✔ What is/has been the biggest problem in regard to…?

✔ What would be the **worst case scenario** if you think about…?

✔ If you think about… or…, which do you like more, which is more **trustworthy**? etc.

## Splitting up the price

A product **appears** more valuable if you explain the individual components that make up the price. This is not about giving the customer a calculation example but to make it clear to him just how many individual benefits and features he is getting.

It is important not **merely** to mention specific characteristics, but all features, even if they meanwhile have become standard features.

 You may handle this situation as follows:

✔ If they are standard features, use phrases such as *"Of course,... is included, too," "Naturally, the product also features...,"* etc.

✔ *Accentuate* fully included auxiliary services by saying *"standard"* or *"even standard."*

✔ Call special features, which the customer normally does not expect or only gets *for a surcharge, "a highpoint," "an outstanding service,"* or *"a special advantage."*

# "You deserve it"

As every salesperson knows, if a customer buys very expensive products for himself, the emotional, rather than the rational, reasons *count*. Still, many customers look for *justification* to explain their decision to themselves and to others. In this situation, you may use phrases that *flatter* the customer's ego. Some examples: *"You've accomplished so much, you're entitled to it," "You're worthy of it," "You deserve that."*

---

## Palabras para recordar

**to mention:** to talk about, to point out, to state, to bring up, to refer to

**to keep in mind:** to remember, to not forget, to take into consideration

**perceived:** sensed, felt

**to make one aware of something:** to make one conscious of or open one's eyes to something

**varied:** diverse, assorted, miscellaneous, diversified

**appropriate:** right, correct, proper, apt

**vital:** very important, essential, imperative, crucial, central

**consist of:** involve, be made up of, include, embody, incorporate

*(continúa)*

## *Continuación*

**to be able to afford something:** to have the funds for, manage to pay for, or find the money for something

**to reward oneself for something:** to give oneself a present for something

**recognition:** acknowledgement, appreciation, applause

**to take a liking to something:** to take pleasure in or enjoy something

**to express:** to demonstrate, to communicate, to exhibit, to indicate

**instance:** case, example, case in point

**gain:** benefit, advantage, reward, profit

**self-esteem:** self-worth, sense of worth, pride in oneself, faith in oneself

**substantiated by:** supported, validated, verified, proven, or backed up by

**slight:** small, minor, little

**resale value:** worth of something being sold again

**durable consumer goods:** long-lasting, hard-wearing, or strong end-user commodities

**preservation of value:** maintenance, continuation, upholding, keeping of worth

**low tendency to break down:** slight inclination or propensity to stop working

**wear and tear:** signs of use, friction, deterioration, damage, or erosion

**rare:** unusual, uncommon, out of the ordinary, exceptional

**collector's value:** saver's or accumulator's worth

**to fetch:** to sell for, to go for, to bring in, to yield

**refurbishing:** renovating, restoring, revamping, overhauling, making over

*(continúa)*

## *Continuación*

**may be created by:** may be produced or generated by, may be a result of

**to constitute:** to represent, to amount to, to add up to, to signify

**storage costs:** warehouse or stockroom expenses

**to induce someone to do something:** to cause, get, or prompt someone to do something

**in favour of:** for, pro, in support of, on behalf of

**to bother:** to disturb, to worry, to concern, to perturb, to trouble, to disconcert

**rather than with:** instead with, more readily than with

**worst case scenario:** most terrible, awful, or unpleasant future situation

**trustworthy:** dependable, reliable

**to appear:** to seem, to give the impression of being

**merely:** just, only, simply

**to accentuate:** to emphasise, to highlight, to underline, to stress

**for a surcharge:** for an additional price, for extra cost

**outstanding:** exceptional, terrific, excellent, great

**you deserve it:** you earn it, you have a right to have it

**to count:** to matter, to be of consequence, to be of account, to make a difference

**justification:** good reason, explanation, rationalisation

**to flatter:** to butter up, to soft-soap, to play up to

**to accomplish:** to achieve, to succeed in, to get done, to pull off

**you are entitled to it:** you are worthy of or qualified for it

# *How* to recognise *buying signals*

Many a business deal has **fallen through** because the salesperson didn't recognise the customer's buying signals.

To sales representative Peter W. from Hannover, a buying signal is already given if the customer is basically willing to look for a product or a solution. However, such an initial buying signal is not yet **related to** a specific **brand** or provider. *"It merely demonstrates that the customer has recognised his requirements and **is very determined to meet** them,"* says the sales representative.

If it is **obvious** that the customer wants to buy, it would be a **mistake** to still try to convince him of the general necessity. At worst, you may get the opposite effect if you do so, *"The customer starts **to reconsider** everything and is beginning to have **doubts** whether the purchase is really necessary,"* explains Peter W.

On the other hand, you can not automatically **assume** that prospective customers, who schedule an initial appointment or who even initiate contact, are really ready to buy. Peter W. gives an example, *"Some customers start early on to collect information about possible solutions, even if the **award of contract** date is still a long way off."* Also, it happens that prospects consult the sales representative in order to find out if a purchase is worthwhile for them or if it would be better to wait until new developments come on the market. *"In this case, of course, you carry the risk of advising the customer free of charge and at the end you **come away empty-handed**,"* says Peter W. Therefore, he always steers the prospect toward his own offer, *"You should not provide too much general information but you should always establish a connection to your product."*

### *Watch for* clues

The biggest challenge is to recognise in time when the customer has made a decision *in favour of* your offer. "You can find that out but watching for clear signs or by asking the customer," says Peter W.

The customer is ready to buy if he *intently concerns himself with* the sales representative's offer and, on his own, lists the advantages. *"It's always a good sign if the customer has invested a lot of time in doing so,"* explains Peter W. Even the question about making a price concession is a *distinct* buying signal. In Peter W.'s experience, this question is usually asked at the close, when the customer has already made the decision and now tries *to gain* further advantages.

If the customer doesn't provide any clear signals, it helps to ask him questions. *It goes without saying* for Peter W. to ask the customer which other suppliers he is in contact with, *"It doesn't make any difference what the customer's reaction is: You can always draw your conclusions. If he is evasive, it is obvious that he compares offers, and if he says 'no' you usually notice if this is true or not."* Definite clues are also if the customer *feels* clearly *uneasy, makes a face* or tries hard to keep a certain look on his face.

## "Grab it" straightaway

If the customer provides clear buying signals (*"Well, everything is alright then," "Yes, that's how we'll do it,"* etc.) you have to *"seize the opportunity immediately,"* says Peter W. In this case, the biggest problem for him is that he, as a sales representative, is sometimes "programmed" differently. *"One assumes that one still has to make this or another sales argument or one reckons that there is going to be an objection. If there is none, one is so dumbfounded that the customer's quick decision seems suspicious."* However, reactions such as *"That was quite a quick decision – it's not a problem if you think it over till tomorrow,"* *are a no-no* for

Peter W. *"That may only happen to you if you're a beginner,"* he says. Sometimes, though, Peter W. has to ***restrain himself*** from following up with more sales arguments.

---

## Palabras para recordar

**to recognise:** to identify, to make out, to spot, to detect, to pinpoint

**to fall through:** to come to nothing, to fail to happen, to not come off, to fall flat

**related to:** connected with, linked to, associated with, affiliated with

**brand:** make, product, trade name, trademark, brand name

**merely:** only, simply, just, purely

**to be very determined:** to be enormously set, bent, or intent

**to meet:** to fulfil, to satisfy, to fill

**obvious:** clear, evident, noticeable, apparent, perceptible

**mistake:** blunder, inaccuracy, miscalculation, slip-up

**to reconsider:** to rethink, to go back over, to re-evaluate, to reassess, to have second thoughts about

**doubts:** a lack of confidence or faith, uneasiness, apprehension, misgivings

**to assume:** to take for granted, to presuppose, to believe, to imagine

**award of contract:** contract award process, placing of orders

**to come away empty-handed:** to miss out, to fail to benefit, to lose out

**clue:** sign, hint, evidence, indication, pointer

**in favour of:** for, pro, in support of, on the side of, giving backing to

*(continúa)*

## *Continuación*

**to intently concern oneself with:** to be very interested in or involved with

**distinct:** clear, unmistakeable, definite, recognisable, palpable, noticeable, plain

**to gain:** to get, to win, to secure, to obtain, to capture, to pick up, to procure

**to go without saying:** to be a given, to be a normal thing, to be completely natural

**to draw one's conclusions:** to come to a deduction, assumption, presumption, or inference

**to be evasive:** to be hard to pin down, vague, equivocal, or indirect

**to feel uneasy:** to feel tense, ill at ease, anxious, apprehensive, uncomfortable, or edgy

**to make a face:** to grimace, to frown, to have a distorted expression, to scowl

**grab it straightaway:** seize the opportunity immediately, at once, right away, or without delay

**to reckon:** to be of the opinion, to believe, to suppose, to surmise, to deem

**to be so dumbfounded:** to be so flab-bergasted, astonished, astounded, taken aback, or stunned

**to seem suspicious:** to appear to be dubious, to give the impression of being suspect

**to be a no-no for someone:** to be a taboo, unmentionable, banned, or prohibited for someone

**to restrain oneself:** to hold back, keep back, contain, or hinder oneself

# Speeding up *decision-making processes*

There are customers who try **to feed a salesperson's hopes** with vague and **meaningless** phrases. Real pros **don't let themselves be put off** by this sort of behaviour.

"We'll get back with you when we've made a decision." – Sales representatives, who **let themselves in for** such "arrangements," might as well forget about closing the sale, Kevin G., a sales representative from Bonn makes clear. Even if the customer explains why he needs more time, Kevin G. knows that a lot can **crop up** during this period. It happened to him once during a phase of non-communication that a competitor aggressively **approached** the customer and **got the bid**, "because he **was virtually ubiquitous**."

## *The danger in having time to think it over*

Kevin G. learned a great deal from this experience and took the necessary steps, *"It's often a matter of* **misconceived** *politeness* **to restrain oneself** *and give the customer time to think about buying. Doing so is very dangerous; you should always try to be present when the customer makes his decision."*

Although he may **come across as pushy** to some customers, Kevin G. **abides by** the motto, *"Better one contact too many than not enough."* While the sales representative initially shows understanding for the customer's request for time, he will **nevertheless** contact him during this phase, *"Then, it becomes obvious right away whether the customer really* **concerned himself with** *the decision or whether he hadn't given it another thought."*

## Stick to your guns

It is useful in both cases to follow up consistently, *"I see it as a clear promise when a customer **assures** me that he will contact me within the next two weeks. If I call him at the beginning of the second week, he realises that I take him at his word. He **feels more obligated** and there is a greater chance that now he will really **go into** my offer,"* says Kevin G. *"On the other hand if you contact the customer after the two weeks are over, he may find excuses why he hasn't looked into the offer. Now you have **to take a new run at it**, set a new **deadline**, etc."*

## Offer support

*"I have to communicate with the customer exactly at the point when he's right in the middle of the decision-making process, because this is a time when **doubts** may come up,"* explains Kevin G. *"During the first presentation, the customer usually has not reached the point where he realises **the full extent** of his decision. Actually, the most critical phase comes afterwards and that's exactly when I need to be there for him to give him the best possible support."* There is another reason why this phase is important: The customer **seeks advice from** a number of people who cannot, in every case, be influenced by the sales representative. "It's relatively easy to identify the co-decision makers in the customer's company. However, it gets difficult if he looks for guidance among his friends, acquaintances, and colleagues, for example at the '**notorious**' golf club," says Kevin G. "At such a place the customer is influenced by a variety of people and it is quite possible that he suddenly changes his mind or **drags out** the decision."

In this situation, the best way, too, is "**to hang on**," as the sales representative calls it, in order not to allow the customer any "**way out**." Kevin G. explains, *"If the customer tells me that he needs two days, I contact him at the end of the second day. If he still needs to clarify something, I inquire what it is and whom the customer will consult. It is my goal, of course,* *to help him realise that it's best that I be present during that discussion."*

---

## Palabras para recordar

**to speed up:** to accelerate, to hurry up

**to feed someone's hopes:** to make empty promises to someone

**meaningless:** valueless, empty, futile

**to not let oneself be put off:** to not let oneself be turned away or brushed off

**to let oneself in for something:** to get involved or caught up in something

**to crop up:** to happen, to occur, to come to pass, to arise

**to approach:** to make advances to, to proposition, to solicit

**to get the bid:** to win the contract

**to be virtually ubiquitous:** to be practically ever-present or omnipresent

**misconceived:** imagined, misinterpreted, misunderstood

**to restrain oneself:** to hold oneself back, to keep oneself in check

**to come across as pushy:** to be perceived as aggressive or forceful

**to abide by:** to follow, to keep to

**nevertheless:** all the same, just the same, in any event, nonetheless

**to concern oneself with something:** to busy oneself with or devote one's time to something

**to stick to one's guns:** to remain firm, resolute, determined, or unwavering

**to assure:** to give one's word to

*(continúa)*

### Continuación

**to feel more obligated:** to feel more compelled, obliged, or duty-bound

**to go into something:** to tackle, deal with, or apply oneself to something

**to take a new run at it:** to try again, to have another go at it

**deadline:** time limit, cut-off-date, target

**doubts:** misgivings, qualms, uncertainties, uneasiness, apprehension

**the full extent:** the complete scale, degree, or magnitude

**to seek advice from:** to consult with

**notorious:** legendary, famous, renowned

**to drag out:** to protract, to draw out

**to hang on:** to hold out, to stay close

**way out:** possibility for escape

# Ready to close the sale?

Whenever a customer is ready to make the buying decision, he will *reveal* it to the salesperson – *provided* he has been asked the right questions.

"Yes, our old copy machine *is prone to breaking down*." To Rank Xerox sales representative Allan G., this sentence, *uttered* during a sales talk, was *a revelation*: The customer had already *made up his mind to* buy. Now, it was just a matter of working out the delivery details.

The American company, Rank Xerox, had more than 12000 of their sales representatives' sales talks evaluated in order *to determine* at what point the customer makes his decision to buy. It was important to this global corporation **to become aware of** this fact because **they knew from experience**: If the sales representative moves to the closing phase too early or too late, chances for making the sale are reduced **considerably**.

If a sales representative **is overly zealous**, he **provokes** a negative reaction because the customer may still **entertain considerable doubt**. However, if he misses the **appropriate** moment to ask the closing question and instead **inundates** the customer with further arguments, he even risks that the customer may ask himself, *"What's wrong here that he's trying so hard to convince me?"*

## Asking the right questions at the right moment

While evaluating the study, the Rank Xerox sales managers **came to an interesting conclusion**: At any time during the sales talk, sales representatives are able to find out if their customers are ready for the closing. All it takes is asking the right questions.

Allan G., whose sales strategy was also analysed in the study, **takes his time** until he asks these "right questions:" *"As long as my customers reply 'yes, but' to each of my answers and keep coming up with a counter argument for each of my arguments, it's clearly too soon to ask them."*

The right time has come when all of the customer's objections have been **resolved** by giving the right answers.

Then, it is just a matter of asking the right questions, for example, *"Your old machine seems prone to breaking down. How frequently does that happen?"*

If the customer replies *"... actually, **it has not failed us yet**,"* Allan G. changes the subject and proceeds to ask another question to test the customer's readiness to close, *"If you compare your machine to **state-of-the-art** models, buying toner **cartridges runs into a lot** *of money*, doesn't it? How high are your **office supply costs**?"

If the customer's reply shows that he still hasn't developed a concrete buying need, Allan G. **broaches** a new subject, which may lead to the closing question, *"These old copy machines allow you to print in black and white only. And if you compare the **printed impression** with those of modern machines … What do you do if you want to copy advertising brochures?"*

If the customer now reacts with a suitable answer, *("That's true, for such tasks we always have to use a copy shop.")* then Allan G. follows up with a whole series of questions, which are **steering** him towards the closing, *"The copy shops are not exactly cheap. How much money do you spend there per month?"* – *"It surely costs you a lot of time to take the thing there and pick it up again. How long does it take your **associate** to get to the copy shop and back?"* – *"How much time does it take your copy shop **to carry out** your order?"*

If the customer's answers show how very dissatisfied he is with his current situation, Allan G. asks the all important closing question, *"Then it would be much quicker and cheaper if you could do such print work on your own copier. If you were able to save 20 % of your printing costs, would that be a reason for you **to substitute** your old black and white copy machine **for** an efficient colour copier?"*

If Allan G. is dealing with especially sceptical customers, he uses "closed" questions **exclusively**, which the customer can only answer with "yes" or "no." Examples: "With your old copy machine, one copy costs … cents, with a new one only … cents. Isn't that a considerable difference?" – "Isn't it **aggravating** that your copy machine breaks down regularly?" – "The repair costs are surely running high?"

The basic idea behind this procedure: Each "yes" from the customer brings the sales representative nearer to his final closing question. Then, it's only a formality for the customer to say "yes" and sign the order.

---

## Palabras para recordar

**to reveal:** to impart, to communicate, to disclose, to divulge

**provided:** as long as, on the condition that, on the assumption that

**to be prone to breaking down:** to be likely, disposed, or predisposed to stop working

**to utter:** to say, to speak, to express, to voice, to state

**a revelation:** an eye-opener, a realisation

**to make up one's mind to do something:** to come to a decision or reach a conclusion to do something

**to determine:** to find out, to discover, to learn, to establish, to ascertain

**to become aware of something:** to know, to be informed of or in the know about something

**they knew from experience:** they had learned or realised from previous incidents

**considerably:** significantly, very much, a great deal, substantially

**to be overly zealous:** to be too hasty, eager, keen, intense, or forceful

**to provoke:** to evoke, to cause, to give rise to, to elicit, to induce

**to entertain considerable doubt:** to harbour scepticism, uneasiness, apprehension, or distrust

**appropriate:** suitable, proper, right, apt, pertinent, opportune

**to inundate:** to overwhelm, to swamp, to overburden, to bog down

*(continúa)*

## *Continuación*

**to convince:** to persuade, to prevail upon, to sway, to coerce

**to come to an interesting conclusion:** to learn of a compelling result or outcome

**to take one's time:** to proceed

**resolved:** answered, sorted out, cleared up

**it has not failed us yet:** it has not let us down or disappointed us so far

**state-of-the-art:** up to date, modern, advanced

**cartridge:** cassette, container

**to run into a lot of money:** to be quite expensive or costly

**office supply costs:** expenses for place of work resources

**to broach:** to bring up, to introduce, to raise, to mention, to open

**printed impression:** print image, printed design

**associate:** colleague, fellow worker, co-worker, employee, member of staff

**to steer:** to guide, to manoeuvre, to lead, to directassociate: assistant, staff member

**to carry out:** to fulfil, to complete, to execute, to finish

**to substitute for:** to replace with, to exchange for, to use instead of, to switch with

**exclusively:** solely, only

**aggravating:** frustrating, irritating, annoying, getting on one's nerves

# Capítulo 2

# Trabajo en equipo y gestión

*U*n buen vendedor debe trabajar en función de las necesidades de sus clientes potenciales. El proceso de venta determina en buena medida el funcionamiento interno de la empresa y la producción. Para que la venta se realice con mayor agilidad hay que saber detectar errores, fijar objetivos y establecer medidas de control sobre todo el proceso productivo.

Todo ello tiene un objetivo: fidelizar al cliente. Sólo hablaremos de una venta exitosa cuando aumente el porcentaje de ventas y, además, tengamos un cliente satisfecho. Si eres capaz de ver más allá de la primera venta, ¡enhorabuena! Habrás hecho un cliente para toda la vida.

# *Market-oriented variant management*

Customers want a ***multifaceted selection*** of products. But a large product range also raises costs.

*"The customer can have any colour he wants so long as it's black"* was Henry Ford's legendary quote when he brought his "Model T" on the market in 1913. Today, in the age of mass customisation, there are ***virtually*** no technical limits for the richness in variance of a product. The ***boundaries***, however, lie in the cost, as corporate consultants Bettina Zimmermann and Sebastian Hohenfeld of Kucher & Partner in Munich explain: *"Customers indeed wish for a large number of differentiated products. But generally, they **are not willing** to pay for extras."*

So variance is turning into a heavy cost factor, the corporate consultants ***illustrate*** by using the example of a parts manufacturer in southern Germany, *"Within eight years, the product mix depth has **quadrupled**. And every parts variance, in its initial creation, is reflected in the budget with 5000 Euros, in addition to higher **storage** costs and **expenses for tied up capital**."*

The solution to this uncontrolled growth of product lines was, until now, standardisation and ***same parts management***. But it is also possible to control product line development via sales measures: *"It is important for the sales manager **to become aware of** the point at which the costumer's benefit and the cost of a product variant **correlate** in a reasonable manner,"* explain the consultants.

For that purpose, an appropriate instrument for analysis is necessary to find out ***to what extent*** the budget ***complies with*** the customers' demands. Bettina Zimmermann and Sebastian Hohenfeld state, as an example, the range of product offers for car interiors: individually adjustable back seats create relatively high costs for the manufacturer, but offer only a relatively small additional benefit to the customer. That is why it can **be neglected** as a variant in the offer.

The sales managers find out how high the customers' benefit is with the help of the so-called **"conjoint measurement"**, the key question being: *"If the customer has a special wish, how much money is he willing to pay to have it fulfilled?"* The **reckoning**: If the client shows a low willingness to pay, the need is low.

## Three essential starting points

In this variant management, there are three starting points: Right at the product launch, only such variants should be offered that the sales department **labels as decisive for success**: *"It is not about the technically doable, but about what the customer needs and what could influence his buying decision,"* the consultants say.

In the second phase, priority is given to "variant **containment**." Thereby, those variants are eliminated that were reported by the sales force as showing a declining demand. And additional variants are created that promise new sales impulses. At the end of the product life cycle, it is purely the budget that is important: Only variants that produced large sales figures are kept.

The reduction of variants, however, **constitutes** a possible risk of losing customers. That is why, with the help of the so-called "customer satisfaction-flexibility-matrix," the consequences of reducing the variants have to be analysed. Consequently, the customer relationship is classified between:

✔ the customer's quality, price, and service needs were fulfilled/not fulfilled and

✔ the customer requires standard products/
individual solutions.

## *Take cues from the targeted customer-segment*

Clear customer segmentation is crucial to success
for intelligent variant management in the opinion of
Bettina Zimmermann and Sebastian Hohenfeld:
*"The stronger a product is oriented towards the requests
of a clearly limited target audience, the fewer **special
requests** are to be expected, because within one
customer segment needs are usually homogeneous."*
Another advantage of this procedure: When needs
change, additional variants do not necessarily have to
be offered. It is enough **to adjust** the existing variants.

## *New pricing strategies*

Intelligent variant management also offers a good
basis for pricing strategies. The so-called "pricedriven
customers" can **help themselves to** the standard
variants. Customers with a high willingness to
pay can be reached through exclusive variants
that initially create higher costs but also allow the
**implementation** of higher prices.

---

### Palabras para recordar

**variant:** variation, modification, option, alternative

**multifaceted:** many-sided, versatile, manifold, all-round

**selection:** assortment, range, variety, choice, mixture

**virtually:** almost, nearly, practically, in effect, as good as,
effectively, next to

**boundary:** border, limit, bounding line, constraint

**to not be willing:** to not be prepared, ready, keen,
agreeable, or disposed

*(continúa)*

## *Continuación*

**to illustrate:** to exemplify, to demonstrate, to show

**to quadruple:** to multiply by four

**storage:** stockroom, storehouse, warehouse, depot

**expenses for tied up capital:** cost of the employed capital, associated costs

**same parts management:** identical, equal, or matching components supervision

**to become aware of:** to consciously register, to realise, to open one's eyes to

**to correlate:** to show a relationship, to draw a parallel, to equate, to associate

**to what extent:** to which degree, amount, level, scope, or point

**complies with:** adheres to, conforms to, acquiesces with, assents to, meets the terms of

**be neglected:** be ignored, looked over, disregarded, forgotten, or avoided

**conjoint measurement:** united, connected, or combined analysis

**reckoning:** estimate, calculation scheme, weighing up

**to label as:** to consider, regard, classify, characterise, or designate as

**decisive for success:** important, crucial, influential, or key for victory

**containment:** control, restriction, regulation, limitation

**to constitute:** to comprise, to represent, to create, to cause to be

**cue:** hint, signal, sign, intimation, indication

**special request:** particular wish, demand, desire, or pleading

*(continúa)*

---

### *Continuación*

**to adjust:** to correct, to fine-tune, to change, to alter, to modify, to amend

**to help oneself to:** to take, to take possession of, to walk off with

**implementation:** pushing through, application, carrying out

## *Classic marketing* traps

*Detecting* corporate mistakes early *prevents* wrong decisions.

Quite a few small and medium-sized companies are *subconsciously* falling into the same traps: Frequently, the much-feared competition *beats you to the punch*, gaining the customer's favour and perhaps even *ruthlessly hijacking* your very own ideas. What is the problem?

Many small and medium-sized businesses are bowing low to the motto: just *don't stand out*. They are afraid of:

- ✔ provoking the competition,
- ✔ being a magnet for buyouts and takeovers,
- ✔ *alluring* intellectual theft,
- ✔ becoming *a victim* of the media,
- ✔ inspiring *jealousy* in their community, etc.

In a safely tucked away and *concealed* niche, life can flash by comfortably by comparison. The *downside* of this, however, is that it will continually become more difficult to attract new customers and to distinguish yourself in a reputable way or for potential customers to even find their way to you, much the same as qualified employees. In the event of an "***incident***," you can be sure of the fact that the press and respectively the public will react far more concerned to such news from an ***unknown entity*** than from an already respected and well-known company!

Textbook trap of the small and medium-sized businesses: not being able to let go. They are afraid of:

> ✔ ***bidding farewell to*** a portion of their customer base:
> ✔ even if it hardly generates any revenue,
> ✔ accumulates high costs and
> ✔ ***jams*** capacities that are essentially needed for expansions and development.

Many small businesses initially start their business activities with only one product or service. After a successful start, variants are developed, new product lines are added and everything broadens instead of striving forward. Often, it is believed that maintaining as many products as possible can generate steady sales or even increase them. But that is a ***fallacy!***

> ✔ Constantly review your product portfolio, looking for the key providers.
> ✔ ***Amply*** practise cost management and use controlling instruments.
> ✔ Aside from revenues, direct your attention to the creation of value, respectively the EBITDA (earnings before ***interest***, taxes, ***depreciation***, and amortisation.)

The ***human resources*** trap: ***hurt no one***. They are afraid of:

> ✔ rearranging the personnel structure regarding executive and employees,
> ✔ because it is often believed that doing so may ***destroy*** the corporate climate, culture, of the existential self-image.

This is *the most malicious* trap yet: Employees and executives have brought the company to the top with team spirit and loyalty.

Yet, this may have led to *subliminal* conflict and resentment amongst them. Executives, who are blocking one another, *constrain* the *desperately needed implementation* of effective marketing strategies far more often *than suspected*.

## So, what can you do?

*Scrutinise* your personal formulas for success regularly and *dispose of* them if needed, when new *necessities* are *emerging* on the horizon. For these decisions you will, above all, need *objective targets* and controlling instruments.

---

### Palabras para recordar

**trap:** pifall, snare, stumbling block, catch

**to detect:** to identify, to catch, to become aware of, to notice, to discern

**to prevent:** to put a stop to, to stave off, to ward off, to block, to thwart, to avoid

**subconsciously:** unknowingly, unwittingly, inadvertently, unintentionally

**to beat one to the punch:** to win the race, to be faster or quicker than oneself

**ruthlessly:** mercilessly, unmercifully, pitilessly, remorselessly

**to hijack:** to take over, to take control of, to seize

**to not stand out:** to not attrack attention or catch the eye

**to allure:** to attract, to draw

**a victim:** an easy prey or target, a drupe

*(continúa)*

## *Continuación*

**jealousy:** envy, resentment, covetousness, resentfulness

**concealed:** hidden, out of sight, unnoticed, obscured

**downside:** disadvantage, danger, drawback, negative consequence

**incident:** unpleasant occurrence or happening

**unknown entity:** unfamiliar organisation or film

**to bid farewell to something:** to de without or give up something

**to jam:** to obstruct, to block, to clog, to congest, to clice off

**fallacy:** misleading notion, erroneous belief, false conclusion, misconception, misjudgement

**amply:** sufficiently, adequately, abundantly

**interest:** dividend, profit, return. percentage gain

**depreciation:** decrease, lowering, or reduction in value

**human resources:** personnel, staff, employees, workers, workforce

**to hurt no one:** to upset, cause sorrow to, or cause anguish to nobody

**to destroy:** to damage, to harm, to impair

**the most malicious:** the most harmful, hurtful, or destructive

**subliminal:** unconscious, hidden, unintentional

**to constrain:** to hinder, to restrict, to hamper, to limit

**desperately needed:** very much, greatly or urgently required

**implementation:** carrying out, realisation, enforcement

**than suspected:** than believed, expected, imagined, supposed, deduced, or guessed

*(continúa)*

| *Continuación* |
| --- |
| **to scrutinise:** to examine, to analyse, to inspect, to go over, to peruse |
| **to dispose of something:** to get rid of something, to clear something out, to leave something behind |
| **necessities:** needs, requirements, requisites, essentials |
| **to emerge:** to appear, to become visible, to surface, to materialise, to come out |
| **objective targets:** aims, goals |

# *Three paths to success*

By restructuring their sales department, Heraeus Kulzer, a *limited liability company, achieved a more customer-friendly approach* at less selling costs.

Up to now, the sales department at Heraeus Kulzer was organised to be product-oriented. *Due to* acquisitions and *mergers*, each product group had its own sales organisations. These led their customers separated from one another into different data bases. For each product group, the goods were offered, shipped, and *invoiced* separately. There was no information exchange at all.

Now, the company, producing chemical materials required for dentistry, has a new *rallying cry*, "One face to the customer." Firstly, they *consolidated* the *distribution channels*, secondly, they stablished a customer service centre, and thirdly, they fed a central "data warehouse" with all the customer information, which *previously* had been collected locally.

The results are intensified customer loyalty and improved customer service as well a reduction in processing costs, as reported by Enrico Senger and

Hubert Österle from the Institute for Information Systems at the University of St. Gallen, who also *oversee* the reorganisation project.

## The background

The industry's ten largest companies, with Heraeus Kulzer being one of them, *share* half of the total market among themselves. Heraeus Kulzer's goal was to expand their market shares. Because there is not much potential for differentiation in the product *range*, the company saw their chance to improve customer service.

The most important step was to separate the sales department by customer groups and *to set up* only one channel of distribution each, which is one for the 8000 dental laboratories and one for the 40 000 dental practices in Germany.

This step also became necessary because the customer groups' shopping *behaviour* has changed. As a rule, dentists purchase their *extensive* materials *wholesale*, at so-called dental depots. Laboratories bundle their requirements via *buying syndicates*, "Therefore, co-ordinated product systems and *simplified procurement* logistics are strong incentives for dental laboratories to order from only one manufacturer," say Enrico Senger and Hubert Österle. "The goal, therefore, was a fully integrated solution *for the purpose of comprehensive* customer relationship management."

The most important tasks in the implementation of "One face to the customer" *consisted of*:

- ✔ Merging and newly *linking* customer data, which had been coming from *various sources*.
- ✔ Establishing the Internet as an additional channel of distribution.
- ✔ Synchronising it with the existing contact channels (multi-channel management).

Thereby the following goals should be reached:

- ✔ Reduction of tasks which *are not adding value*.
- ✔ Elimination of *superfluous* transactions.
- ✔ Possibility for the creation of customer profiles and for customer segmentation.
- ✔ Implementation of segment-specific sales and marketing activities.

## Two criteria for measuring success

Whether the sales department's restructuring is taking a successful course should be determined *mainly* by using two measuring criteria, which are:

- ✔ an increase in the percentage of sales,
- ✔ an increase in customer satisfaction.

The measuring criteria "cost reduction," however, was *abandoned* because in the opinion of the person in charge there is a risk that it may come into conflict with the main goals. To project manager Oliver Assmus, chief of Heraeus Kulzer's customer service centre, the *inclusion* of the customers' requirements was an essential factor for success. Therefore, customers of the different segments were asked about their needs.

The implementation of the CRM solution was done step-by-step but simultaneously for all distribution channels. The critical point for success was the sales force's involvement, report Enrico Senger and Hubert Österle, *"It was important to make it clear to 120 sales representatives that a reorganisation was also in their best interest. The project team was **considering** a special incentive system. As it turned out, **equipping** the sales force with laptops was already incentive enough. But it **was even more essential to firmly root** customer relationship management in their mentality."*

The *core* of the new organisation is the newly created customer service centre, *"Instead of having to identify* *and call the individual product group contacts, the customer may now contact us by calling a **toll-free service number**.*" However, a ***prerequisite*** for the successful restructuring was that the sales team acquire broad product knowledge. Another factor for success consisted in ***recruiting*** associates for the customer service centre who were already equipped with the necessary expertise, such as former dentist's assistants.

## Palabras para recordar

**path:** way, road, avenue, route

**limited liability company:** corporation, private limited company

**to achieve:** to accomplish, to pull off, to arrive at, to attain, to procure

**a more customer-friendly approach:** an extra client-responsive manner or style

**due to:** because of, owing to, by reason of, as a result of, caused by

**merger:** amalgamation, fusion, joining, combination, union

**invoiced:** billed, charged, debited

**rallying cry:** slogan, catchword, motto

**to consolidate:** to combine, to merge, to unite, to join, to fuse, to amalgamate

**distribution channels:** sales means, media, vehicles, or routes

**previously:** before, until that time, earlier on, in the past, formerly, until then

**to oversee:** to supervise, to run, to watch over, to manage, to direct

**to share:** to divide up, to split

**range:** assortment, variety, array, choice

*(continúa)*

## *Continuación*

**to set up:** to establish, to create, to get going, to start, to institute

**behaviour:** activities, conduct, manners

**extensive:** large-scale, substantial, considerable

**wholesale:** in bulk, in large quantities

**buying syndicate:** purchasing association or group

**simplified:** easier, simpler, streamlined, reduced to essentials

**procurement:** purchasing, resource acquisition

**for the purpose of:** as defined by, in the sense of

**comprehensive:** all-inclusive, all-embracing, wide-ranging, exhaustive

**to consist of:** to entail, to involve, to include, to comprise, to be composed of

**to link:** to connect, to bring together

**various sources:** a variety of, a range of, different, assorted, or mixed origins

**to not be adding value:** to not be increasing or augmenting worth

**superfluous:** unnecessary, needless, unneeded, not required, redundant

**mainly:** largely, chiefly, mostly, for the most part, primarily, chiefly, principally

**abandoned:** dropped, done without, given up, put aside, relinquished

**inclusion:** incorporation, integration

**to consider:** to think about, to give thought to, to contemplate

**to equip:** to provide, to furnish, to supply, to endow

*(continúa)*

### Continuación

**to be even more essential:** to be all the more important, crucial, or necessary

**to firmly root:** to securely anchor, to strongly embed

**core:** centre, focal point, central part

**toll-free:** free of charge, at no cost, without charge

**prerequisite:** requirement, necessity, precondition

**to recruit:** to hire, to sign up, to take on, to enlist, to enrol

# Top or flop?

In the introductory phase, it is often *determined* whether a product strategy is really competitive and marketable.

The higher the degree of *newness* for a product – meaning a *genuine* innovation *instead of* a me-too-product – the better the chance for the company *to gain* an exclusive and monopolistic competitive advantage on the market. But this competitive lead will most likely *decrease* at some point. In most cases, the great white hope of future sales is being successfully imitated by the competition only after a short while or a similar product *undercuts* the price. So, what can you do?

A great number of companies try *to ward off* imitators with the help of patents and competition laws. This is achieved, for example, by binding or *cutting off* suppliers with agreements to deal exclusively with one business partner in certain types of transactions. Therefore, the product's innovative results can be *kept up* over a certain period of time.

Other companies, for example, design or build the machines necessary for manufacturing on their own, a process that is capital intensive as well as risk intensive, especially in markets with high flop rates.

Simultaneously, the introductory phase **marks** the path of the highest market resistance in a product's life cycle, which generally **is less of a concern** for me-too-products and much more **pronounced** for genuine innovations. Such initial market introduction barriers **need to be prevailed over**.

This can be achieved with the help of strategic partnerships or distributions channels like e-commerce. Because the Internet **enables** companies **to overcome** traditional barriers in a way like never before possible. The size advantage of a company is playing a much smaller role nowadays.

A successful market introduction is often accompanied by a general communications concept that is supposed to create demand in the relevant target group. The USP (unique selling proposition) must be carried by the advertising instruments, by public relations and on to the sales force in their talks with customers. The following **is accomplished**: the message can be transported to the "relevant set" of the target audience faster (*"When I think of a specific product result, I buy product x."*) **Consequently**, the **utmost** creative staging of the advertising message will certainly award the product more **attention** as well as **desire** and supply the necessary push for a placing in the market. Added rebates or extras **ease** the entry into the market.

Yet way too often, **measures** of product introduction still end at the **checkout**. Once initial sales are **hauled in**, the so-called "sales aftercare" (an important value creation element!), meaning the customer care in the post-acquisition and usage phase, is still not paid enough attention to. Here too lies great potential to successfully **distinguish oneself from** the competitors. For some manufacturers, these after-sales revenues and the resulting cash flow are essential for **survival**.

As they say: The first product is sold by the sales representative, the second one by service.

---

## Palabras para recordar

**to determine:** to settle, to decide,

**newness:** inventiveness, freshness, innovation, originality, novelty

**genuine:** indisputable, true, actual, legitimate, real, valid

**instead of:** as an alternative to, as a substitute for, as a replacement for

**to gain:** to achieve, to attain, to reach

**to decrease:** to diminish, to decline, to dwindle, to shrink, to fall, to lessen

**to undercut:** to undersell, to beat, to charge less than, to underbid, to best

**to ward off:** to fend off, to beat off, to stave off, to avert, to rule out, to repel, to repulse, to keep at bay, to fight off

**to cut off:** to break off, to disconnect, to suspend, to discontinue, to intercept

**to keep up:** to maintain, to sustain, to preserve, to uphold, to retain

**to mark:** to indicate, to point to, to show

**to be less of a concern:** to be not as much a cause of worry or unease

**pronounced:** apparent, distinct, evident

*(continúa)*

## *Continuación*

**need to be prevailed over:** must be surmounted, overcome, or conquered

**to enable:** to allow, to entitle, to empower, to make it possible for, to permit

**to overcome:** to conquer, to surmount, to rise above, to prevail over

**is accomplished:** is achieved, pulled off, realised, or brought about

**consequently:** as a result, so, therefore, hence, subsequently

**utmost:** greatest, highest, maximum

**attention:** awareness, consideration, notice, regard, recognition, heed

**desire:** want, longing, craving, yearning

**to ease:** to simplify, to facilitate, to expedite, to clear the way for, to help

**measures:** actions, courses of action, proceedings, steps, means

**checkout:** cash point, cash register

**to haul in:** to pull in, to bring in, to rake in, to generate

**to distinguish oneself from someone:** to differentiate oneself from someone

**survival:** continuation, endurance

# Diligence *and* consistency *lead to success*

Successful time management **demands** two things: A clear, realistic strategy, and a consistent *implementation*.

In practice, strategic time management is implemented only sporadically. But as long as salespeople aren't clear about what their priorities are and as long as they don't determine concretely what is really important and **takes precedence**, they will not even **attempt to tackle** certain projects.

One typical example, noted by Dr. Ewald Lang, trainer and management consultant from Munich, is the acquisition of new customers. Prospecting demands a great deal of time and effort and takes a while till success **ensues**. Therefore, one **is greatly tempted** to return to short-term "success" by continuing to generate sales with the existing customers.

However, to set clear priorities means making a decision, which is best done together with the sales manager within the **target agreement**. The closer the communication and the more regular feedback is given, the better the sales manager will be able to support the sales force in reaching their goals.

For example, if there is an agreement that the sales representative wins over a certain number of new customers and if this goal has top priority, it clearly has to show up in the time management planning. After all the tasks have been planned and scheduled, the next step is the most important one: the implementation. In this case, success depends on **simple virtues**, such as diligence, consistency, and discipline.

Conclusion: "*A diligent salesperson will always achieve better results – even if he may not be a 'natural sales talent.' The more consistent and disciplined he **sticks to his set objectives**, the more successful he will be*," says Dr. Ewald Lang.

Know what's stopping you. The best time management is useless if "*something always **keeps cropping up***." Dr. Ewald Lang summarises the reasons why we often **procrastinate**:

✔ If the goal is still a long time away, actions are moved to the back burner. Solution: Move up the dates for action or **commit yourself** to **partial** steps and goals and control if the partial goals have been reached.

✔ The fear of tackling something new. Solution: Consider what would be the worst that could

## *Assigning* priorities

Assign priorities to all upcoming activities, for example prospecting, **recapturing** lost customers and servicing current customers. Then, **allot** percentages to your priorities **in accordance with** how much time you want to spend on each task. It is important that your planning be realistic: Fixed appointments and time periods, for example **recurring** weekly meetings, consultations with the internal sales force, office work, etc. have to be determined as fixed time blocks. Then, determine the time you want to spend on the individual priorities. This may, for example, result in the following weekly schedule: 2 days for prospecting, 0,5 days for recapturing lost customers, 1,5 days for **attending to** current customers. The extra day, for example, could be your office day on which, of course, you'll be also integrating your tasks. It is important that you inform your colleagues about your fixed times and days. For example, the internal sales force or the call centre, which schedules your appointments, needs to know which days are open for visiting potential customers and which day you have designated to be your office day.

happen and then put the worst case in relation to the actual experience.

✔ *The fear of failing* and *experiencing defeat*. Solution: Make it clear to yourself that it is much worse not to do anything. Only this is defeat.

✔ *Clinging to* what you are familiar with because you know that you can do it well. If things have gone well so far, you *lack the motivation* to make changes. Solution: Make it clear to yourself that new goals open new perspectives.

✔ A lack in motivation – there are no (negative) consequences if you do not tackle the task. Therefore, one doesn't do anything about it and everything goes on as it did before. Solution: Accept motivational incentives, e.g. *along the lines* of variable *remuneration*.

## Palabras para recordar

**diligence:** assiduity, industriousness, heedfulness, laboriousness, conscientiousness

**consistency:** constancy, steadiness, stability, dependability

**to demand:** to require, to need, to necessitate, to call for, to involve

**implementation:** fulfilment, execution, carrying out, realisation

**to take precedence:** to come first, to take priority, to be considered most critical

**to attempt:** to try, to make an effort, to endeavour, to strive, to venture

**to tackle:** to busy oneself with, to apply oneself to, to take on, to get to work at

**to ensue:** to follow, to develop, to come to pass, to occur, to happen, to transpire

*(continúa)*

## *Continuación*

**to be greatly tempted:** to be very much at risk, provoked, or enticed

**target agreement:** contract on objectives or goals

**simple virtues:** straightforward merits, assets, or good qualities

**to stick to one's set objectives:** to adhere to one's determined goals or targets

**to keep cropping up:** to continue to happen, to get in the way, to occur, to turn up

**to procrastinate:** to postpone or delay action, to move action to the back burner

**to commit oneself to:** to promise, obligate, or dedicate oneself to

**partial:** fractional, limited, fragmentary

**fear of failing:** worry about not succeeding, falling short, or not making the grade

**to experience defeat:** to encounter setback or disappointment

**to cling to:** to stick to, to hold to, to abide by, to adhere to

**to lack the motivation:** to not have, be deficient in, or be short of the enthusiasm

**along the lines:** within the framework or bounds, in the context

**remuneration:** compensation, salary, payment

**to assign:** to allocate, to dole out, to distribute, to dispense, to apportion

**to recapture:** to bring back, to return with, to go and get, to get hold of, to win back, to regain, to recover, to reclaim

**to allot:** to apportion, to allocate, to designate, to give, to appropriate

*(continúa)*

*Continuación*

**in accordance with:** in agreement, conformity,
or compliance with

**recurring:** repeated, habitual, regular, continual, returning

**to attend to:** to take care of, to deal with, to give one's
attention to

# Approach *service creatively*

Customers like businesses that find creative answers
and solutions for their needs.

Every single contact with a customer presents you
with an opportunity to be creative, but you also ought
to creatively develop your long-term strategies for
better service.

Some tips for further practical steps:

✔ *Compose* a list of all your routine *behaviour
patterns* regarding your customer relationship
(for example, *predetermined words of
salutation*, standard letters, etc.).

✔ Try to break the routine with creative behaviour
that shows the customers how much you
*appreciate* them!

✔ *Review* all the initiatives that you and
your employees have displayed towards your
customers during the past weeks. Try
*to determine* what impression you might
have left.

Creative managers regularly conduct brainstorming
sessions with their teams to develop new ideas.
Beforehand, it has to be made absolutely clear
that such meetings proceed *devoid of* restrictions,
negativity, *assessments*, and criticism.

These criteria should be measured against the analysis:

✔ Is the idea *unique*?

✔ What is your *gut-feeling* regarding this idea?

✔ Does this idea fit your customer and is it worth developing?

✔ What are you trying *to achieve* by implementing this idea?

While routine *devalues* the relationship with your customer, creativity *valorises* it. Creativity enables you to give more than you are contractually *obliged* to do. That way you can be a step ahead of the competition and other market participants.
This is often achieved easier than believed.

---

### Palabras para recordar

**to approach:** to set about, to tackle, to deal with, to handle

**to compose:** to create, to write, to compile, to make up

**behaviour pattern:** way of acting, system of conduct, comportment, deportment, or bearing

**predetermined:** predecided, fixed, set, pre-planned, pre-set

**words of salutation:** getting or welcome phrases

**to appreciate someone:** to value, esteem, or think highly of someone

**to review:** to re-examine, to reassess, to have another look at, to make another study of

**to determine:** to find out, to clarify, to ascertain, to establish

**devoid of:** without, with no, lacking, free from

**assessment:** judgement, gauging, rating, appraisal, evaluation

**unique:** only one of its kind, exceptional, inimitable, without equal, unmatched

*(continúa)*

### Continuación

**gut-feeling:** guess, hunch, instinct, intuition

**to achieve:** to accomplish, to reach, to realise, to gain

**to devalue:** to diminish, to detract from, to fail to recognise, to bring down

**to valorise:** to enhance, to improve, to boost, to enrich, to reinforce

**obliged:** required, obligated, called-for, compelled

# After the visit is before the visit

They may often **be bothersome**, but meaningful **call reports** help ensure better customer care and make preparation for your next visit much easier.

Sales representatives who **procrastinate in** writing their call reports aren't doing themselves a favour, because the "fresher" the experiences are in your mind the easier it is to put them on paper. Besides, there is less danger in forgetting important things.

 Your call reports must contain the following points:

✔ What type of visit was it (for example, routine visit, cold call, first visit, follow-up visit)?

✔ What was the goal/purpose of your visit (for example, **to explore** the chances for collaboration, to get to know the decision makers, to present a requested offer, etc.)?

✔ Who was present? What is their function? In what way or how strongly do they influence the buying decision?

✔ What were the results? Which agreements were reached?

# Personal *evaluation*

Your call reports should also include your personal evaluation of the following questions:

✔ How was the atmosphere during the talk?

✔ How does the customer *view* your company and your products?

✔ How high do you think the chances are for winning the customer and *retaining* him (if this is a potential customer)?

✔ How do you judge the stability and *durability* of the relationship with the customer (if this is an existing customer)?

✔ Do you notice anything unusual or strange, perhaps some changes, an improvement, or *a change for the worse*?

✔ How do you assess the customer's current situation, his own position in the market and the economic trend?

---

✔ Did you reach the goal you aimed at? If not: What are, in your opinion, the reasons for that?

✔ Which follow-up measures should take place/ were agreed on? Who takes the initiative/is *responsible for* them? By what date?

✔ Which actions must follow immediately?

✔ What other persons are involved/have to be included?

## Palabras para recordar

**to be bothersome:** to be troublesome, inconvenient, incommodious, or annoying

**call report:** account, statement, or description of a sales visit

**to procrastinate in doing something:** to put off, delay, postpone, or adjourn doing something

*(continúa)*

---

### Continuación

**to explore:** to investigate, to examine, to look into, to inquire into

**to be responsible for something:** to be accountable for or in charge of something

**evaluation:** assessment, appraisal, estimation

**to view:** to regard, to think about, to feel about, to perceive, to deem

**to retain:** to keep, to keep hold of, to hold on to

**durability:** permanence, durableness, long-lastingness, soundness

**a change for the worse:** a deterioration, decline, or weakening

---

# The best way to follow up on your customer calls

After the appointment is before the appointment, that is to say that the **utmost** care and attention **is to be executed** before as well as after all sales calls – sales representatives who act **according to** this rule stand the best chances of doing great business with their customers.

Since Gerald E., a sales representative from Hamburg, **cut down** the number of his customer calls, he was able **to greatly amplify** the number of his orders as well as the **revenue**. The reason for this was, *"My appointment book used to be **full to the brim**. But often I didn't have the time to do the necessary follow-up work and keep in touch with prospective customers. I was always behind schedule with my call reports."*

Because his colleagues were all dealing with **similar issues**, they explained to their sales manager that things could not keep going in such a manner, *"We all sat down one Friday afternoon and discussed, until late in the evening, what could be changed."*

The most important conclusion was: The sales representatives don't have to fill every free minute with customer calls but they **are obligated**, however, to prepare and follow up with sales calls according to **binding guidelines**.

Here are **the most notable** rules:

✔ On the day of the customer visit, the sales representative documents which goals were achieved. He is transferring that information via his notebook to company headquarters, at which point the documentation is greatly aided by a structured input system. Should important information be missing, he is advised by the system with an error message and is prompted **to complete** the data.

✔ The sales representative is obligated **to determine** and schedule all follow-up activities. This involves the preparation of offers, follow-up phone calls and all other follow-up activities. He will also establish who will **embark on** such activities and take general control.

✔ In case an acquisition **is abandoned** or **put on the backburner**, the sales representative must **provide** a **compelling** argument for this in the database.

✔ If the customer call leads to a sale, the salesperson is required **to enter into** the database the exact time at which he will recontact the customer. He also determines who will **be in charge of** the after sales service.

Conclusion: By means of the immediate after-care and the binding scheduling and control, it is **ascertained** that prospective customers are being cared for in the best possible **fashion** and, ideally, can be led to close the deal. At the same time, **vital** customer information can be recorded in the database so that it ***is readily available*** for all the ***involved*** employees in the company.

---

## Palabras para recordar

**call:** visit, appointment

**utmost:** greatest, highest, maximum

**is to be executed:** is to be carried out, accomplished, or achieved

**according to:** in keeping with, in accordance with, in agreement with

**to cut down:** to reduce, to decrease

**to greatly amplify:** to significantly increase, augment, boost, or magnify

**revenue:** income, return, yield

**full to the brim:** filled up, full to capacity

**similar issues:** much the same problems, concerns, or difficulties

**to be obligated:** to be required, compelled, obliged, or duty-bound

**binding guidelines:** compulsory, obligatory, or requisite rules

**the most notable:** the most noteworthy, important, or significant

**to complete:** to finish off, to make perfect, to add the finishing or final touch to

**to determine:** to settle on, to fix, to decide, to agree on, to establish

**to embark on:** to set out on, to tackle, to enter on, to take up, to engage in

**something is abandoned:** something is stopped, given up, or dispensed with

*(continúa)*

---

### *Continuación*

**to put on the back burner:** to put on ice, to postpone,
to defer, to put off

**to provide:** to give, to offer, to present

**compelling:** convincing, powerful

**to enter into:** to record in, to put in, to write in, to document in

**to be in charge of something:** to be in command of,
in control of, or responsible for something

**ascertained:** ensured, made sure

**fashion:** way, manner, mode, method

**vital:** very important, critical, imperative

**to be readily available:** to be promptly, quickly, or at once
accessible

**involved:** associated, participating

# *Set goals and priorities*

What takes priority? What has to be done today
until what time? What can wait? When calculating
and structuring the day, do include **buffer times**.
No one can work for four hours **straight**. After
maximally 120 minutes, mind and body **demand** a
short pause. The phase of regeneration often does
not take longer than 10 minutes.

To get everything done in the day and **not be
completely done in** at the end of it, you should
calculate 60 % of your time for active work and leave
a 20 % buffer for unforeseeable events. The remaining
20 % should be used for creative freedom, experts
recommend. Because no one will **climb the social
ladder** by getting done only what they are required to
do anyway.

Another advantage: To set goals and priorities **unburdens** the mind and also motivates. Everything that **can be marked off** during the course of the day is a success.

---

## Palabras para recordar

**buffer times:** leeway, elbowroom, latitude, room to move, breathing space

**straight:** non-stop, without interruption or break

**to demand:** to require, to need, to necessitate, to want, to call for, to cry out for

**to not be completely done in:** to not be utterly exhausted, worn out, tired out, beat, or fatigued

**to climb the social ladder:** to get ahead, to get somewhere, to rise in the world

**to unburden:** to relieve, to soothe, to ease, to alleviate, to mitigate, to assuage

**can be marked off:** can be finished, completed, done, concluded, accomplished, or fulfilled

---

# Customers, associates, and partners in the same boat

The **drugstore chain** dm-group presents itself as an **exemplary** partner of customers, associates, and suppliers. The company **substantiates** its **high repute** with extensive **corporate citizenship**.

Since the company was founded 32 years ago, orientation toward customers and associates has been the top priority for the dm-group, one of the leading drugstore chains in Germany, Austria, Italy, Hungary, and some other European countries. To stay in that position, the company invests greatly in the improvement of what it has to offer: That the company is always willing to listen to the customers' wishes *is exemplified by* the chain's efforts in point-of-sale research. In the past years, the stores were continually optimised and designed more customer-friendly with the assistance of *renowned* market research institutes. The shopping atmosphere in the dm stores is an important component in the company's POS concept. Everything, *from floor to ceiling, is geared towards conveying* a harmonious impression. *Seasonably* changing ceiling decorations *complement* the shop windows' motifs. Spotlights transmit different colours, and sporadic spectral light which *adapts* in colour to the respective season, *is supposed to* provide a pleasant atmosphere. The *reward* for such efforts: Commercial experts from AC Nielsen confirmed to the dm drugstores last year to have the most loyal customers. According to the researchers' study, dm customers spend significantly more money for drugstore products in "their" market than the customers of the competition chains, Schlecker and Rossmann. Another analysis, the "shopper study" conducted by Procter&Gamble, *gives dm similarly high marks*, just as a study about the competitive environment in drugstores, conducted by Lever Fabergé.

*To embrace* the consumers' problems – that is the quintessence of dm's customer principles: *"We aim to distinguish ourselves in the eyes of our customers from our competitors. We do so by using all appropriate marketing tools in order to win consciously-buying, regular customers whose needs are meliorated with our range of products and services offered."* The in-house bio-brand Alverde (this is also the name of dm's customer magazine) builds a bridge between products and the company's longstanding and extensive social engagement: dm, for example, started a *concerted effort* with the German Aids Foundation or supports the foreign aid association Sekem. For such activities, dm's chief executive officer, Professor Götz W. Werner, was decorated last year with the *Federal Cross of Merit*.

It's part of the corporate strategy, that in addition to all these efforts, dm interacts especially well with its associates and business partners. *"Although customer orientation is considered to be the dominating factor in all activities, also required is an equally **substantial** consideration for and support of associate orientation,"* **is the gist of what** has been written in an internal paper. Each associate is **to be "perceived objectively** in his job."** dm attaches great importance to a ***trusting***, good relationship with its business partners. By means of a ***questionnaire***, suppliers as well as dm regularly submit their ***assessment of collaboration***. Evaluated, for example, is ***accessibility***, the completeness of information, or cooperation when new products or services are launched.

---

## Palabras para recordar

**associate:** colleague, fellow worker, co-worker, employee, member of staff

**drugstore chain:** chemist's shop franchise or group

**exemplary:** excellent, commendable, very good, model, ideal

**to substantiate:** to give substance to, to demonstrate, to corroborate

**high repute:** good name, high standing or stature, good reputation

**corporate citizenship:** social and cultural involvement (of businesses)

**to be exemplified by:** to be demonstrated, shown, or represented by

**renowned:** famous, distinguished, well-known, prominent, established

**from floor to ceiling:** from the ground to the roof, from the bottom up

**to be geared towards:** to be aimed at, to work toward

**to convey:** to get across, to communicate, to put across

*(continúa)*

## *Continuación*

**seasonably:** appropriate to the time of the year

**to complement:** to go well with, to be the perfect addition to

**to adapt:** to change, to alter, to modify

**is supposed to:** is meant, intended, or designed to

**reward:** recompense, remuneration, bonus, prize

**to give someone similarly high marks:** to give someone likewise excellent grades or scores

**to embrace:** to accept, to adopt

**to aim:** to aspire, to intend, to want

**to distinguish oneself from:** to set oneself apart from, to separate oneself from

**consciously:** knowingly, wilfully

**to be meliorated:** to be refined, fine-tuned, perfected, or honed

**concerted effort:** combined, joint, or collaborative operation

**Federal Cross of Merit:** one of the highest honours the Federal Republic of Germany awards

**substantial:** sizable, generous, significant, real, weighty, major

**is the gist of what:** is the general idea, essence, or quintessence of what

**to be perceived objectively:** to be seen neutrally or without bias or prejudice

**trusting:** trustful, reliable, dependable

**questionnaire:** survey, opinion poll

**assessment of collaboration:** evaluation of teamwork or partnership

**accessibility:** approachability, availability

# Capítulo 3

# Vender en inglés

- - - - - - - - - - - - - - - - - - - - -

### En este capítulo

- ► Ventas en el extranjero
- ► Abrir nuevos mercados
- ► Analizar y seleccionar clientes

- - - - - - - - - - - - - - - - - - - - -

Abrir un nuevo mercado entraña muchos riesgos, pero es una decisión imprescindible para el crecimiento de la empresa. En un primer momento te sentirás perdido, porque se te escaparán muchos factores relevantes. En este capítulo te enseñaremos a moverte como pez en el agua en este entorno difícil. Aprenderás a seleccionar vendedores en el país escogido, sabrás qué productos y servicios debes vender y, no menos importante, analizarás qué clientes te convienen.

Para ser un buen vendedor tienes que saber qué estás vendiendo y a quién se lo vendes, pero no te olvides de algo no menos importante: ¡debes saber dónde hacerlo! Conocer la idiosincrasia del país donde vas a instalarte es, prácticamente, una garantía de éxito.

# *Selling across borders*

When dealing with foreign customers, it is ideal to speak their language, yet it is especially important *to attune to* their *mindset*.

Normally, aside from the spoken word, there are *grave* differences in the rules of the game regarding business and society, mentality and manners that need to be overcome. Even when *displaying extra caution*, mistakes are often made, mostly *stemming from* lack of knowledge *with regard to* attitude and behaviour.

## *Recruiting salespersons from the target country*

For international business, it *is more sensible* to attract employees that *are natives of* the target country. An example for this is a medium-sized machine builder *from the vicinity of* Darmstadt. He *preferentially assigns* internships to students that *hail from* Poland or the Czech Republic. They in turn assist him when he visits customers in Kattowitz or Pilsen. The *entrepreneur's* goal: He is *tapping* sales talents for the Eastern European markets who are capable of adjusting easily to the mindset of their fellow countrymen.

It is popular practise *to appoint* a local partner as a *principal agent* in the target country. Then it is their mission *to weave* a nationwide network with other commercial agents.

## *Reciprocal advantage*

This exact path, for example, was ventured on by the "Mini Mundus Hobby GmbH," a manufacturer of collectable miniatures from Dreieich in Hessen. The medium-sized company had made the decision **to gain traction on** the American continent. For this purpose, Barbara Elster, an American who is already selling similar products in the United States, **was commissioned** to take over the chief agency.

The cooperation proves to be worthwhile for both: With Barbara Elster, the German company acquired a sales partner who is familiar with the American way of life and who is already collaborating with many American commercial agents. And Barbara Elster gained a new and **sales-boosting** product line for her sales network.

## Master-franchising for quick market success

Franchise systems are a good solution when foreign markets need to be tapped in the shortest time possible. In this case, it is not a chief agent but a master **franchisee**, who is building a sales network for his client.

An example for this is "Eurologos," a service provider from Brussels. The company had set the goal to establish a global network of translation bureaus within a few years, relates CEO Franco Troiano. The core of his success strategy was to find **a seasoned pro** in the **respective** target country, who would be able to build and manage a franchise system there, *"Someone who speaks the language, knows the business ways and **is in touch with** the markets there,"* says Troiano.

The result: Within a few years, the company was able to establish itself in 30 countries and is going on 100 countries by the end of this year.

## Palabras para recordar

**across borders:** in foreign, far-off, or distant countries, overseas

**to attune to:** to adjust to, to adapt to, to familiarise oneself with

**mindset:** way of thinking, attitude, mentality, frame of mind

**grave:** vital, crucial, critical, serious, significant

**to display extra caution:** to show evidence of added carefulness, attention, heed, watchfulness, or concern

**to stem from something:** to arise from, originate from, be rooted in, or derive from something

**with regard to:** concerning, about, on the subject or matter of, as regards

**to be more sensible:** to be more judicious, sagacious, prudent, perceptive, or farsighted

**to be a native of:** to be a citizen or national of

**from the vicinity of:** from the surrounding area, neighbourhood, locality, or district of

**to preferentially assign:** to make a point of allocating, allotting, giving, or apportioning

**to hail from:** to come from, to be a native of, to be born in, to have one's roots in

**entrepreneur:** businessman, business owner, enterpriser

**to tap:** to draw on, to use, to make use of, to utilise, to put to use, to exhaust, to exploit

**to appoint:** to designate, to nominate, to select, to choose, to settle on, to decide on

**principal agent:** chief or general representative

**to weave:** to create, to put together, to contrive, to make up, to fabricate

**reciprocal:** mutual, give-and-take, joint, shared, equal, corresponding

*(continúa)*

## *Continuación*

**to gain traction on:** to establish oneself on, to gain access to the market on, to break into the market on

**was commissioned:** was authorised, empowered, or accredited

**sales-boosting:** sales-increasing, improving, amplifying, enlarging, expanding, or advancing

**franchisee:** one who is given a warrant, charter, or license

**a seasoned pro:** an experienced, a well versed, an established, or a practised specialist

**respective:** particular, specific, individual

**to be in touch with something:** to be familiar with, no stranger to, or accustomed to something

# *Selling products and services simultaneously*

Especially clever salespeople offer not just products to their customers but also the ***matching*** services. This is how René Frauenkron goes about it.

René Frauenkron, a salesman from Bochum, ***has come up with*** an especially useful business idea for his company Boga GmbH. He sells ***deep-frying*** oil to his restaurant and catering business customers and at the same time offers his services ***to dispose of*** the ***used-up*** oil.

It was this combination of products and services offered that ***enabled*** Frauenkron ***to put his competitors in their place***. While others ***have to grapple with*** their customers' ***"stinginess is cool"*** mentality, he is profiting from his customers' ***indolence***, *"They don't have to worry about a thing.*

*I collect their used-up deep-frying oil and at the same time deliver fresh supplies."*

## Quicker than the copy-cats

However, René Frauenkron knew that it takes more than an attractive selling idea *to open up* a new market. Good ideas get copied. Therefore, he had to ask himself, *"What can I do to have the cake before the others divide it among themselves?"* He found the right solution, *"Restaurateurs are a world in themselves. They know one another, they meet and **compare notes**."* Frauenkron **took advantage of** this network for opening up his market.

First of all, he needed a suitable *referral* customer. His objective was to find a local restaurant/catering business with a good reputation. Therefore, he first *approached* the catering department of Schalke 04, a German national league soccer club. There he quickly found good contacts, *"I'm coming from the catering business myself. That's why our meeting was less a sales representative/customer business negotiation than a visit among colleagues."* Another factor, which led to Schalke's quickly placing confidence in René Frauenkron was the competence he displayed while explaining his services, *"My contacts were enthusiastic about my idea. Less than an hour later **it was a done deal**."*

## Successful referral strategy

This successful key-account acquisition provided Frauenkron with the necessary confidence to contact other potential key accounts. His referral strategy *bore fruit* relatively quickly: From the Maritim Hotel Gelsenkirchen, he was referred to the Maritim Hotel Niendorf and from there to the Maritim Hotel Cologne.

Frauenkron reached his goal of opening up the market as quickly as possible via referral customers, *"About 60% of my customers come from referrals."*

During the first month, he had already acquired 20 key accounts, by the second month there were 40, in the third month 60, and today, four years after the start, there are 300. They ***bless*** Frauenkron, who meanwhile has become a franchise partner of Berlin-based "Gerlicher Fette und Öle GmbH," with sales of approximately 600 000 Euros.

## *Profitable additional businesses*

Long since, Frauenkron has expanded his ***line of goods*** and sells, aside from oils and fats, restaurant/catering business ***accessories*** to his colleagues. Every visit to a customer provides him with the opportunity to generate lucrative additional business, *"We talk about the industry and the colleagues and ultimately about what else the customer could use."*

Through all of this, René Frauenkron makes sure to avoid putting pressure on his customers, *"My customers are **old hands** in their business. You **can't pull the wool over their eyes** and you can't talk them into things. You have to convince them what the best solution is for them."*

That he's on the right path ***became obvious*** when the first competitors tried to copy Frauenkron's idea. He reacted promptly, *"I went a step further and turned it into a **reusable** system, using the delivery canisters also for the disposal of used-up oils."*

Conclusion: By offering his combined product/services strategy, René Frauenkron managed to keep 93 out of 100 new customers, *"If something runs smoothly and serves his convenience, the customer stays with it, and it doesn't matter if the competition tries **to tempt** him with low prices."*

## Palabras para recordar

**matching:** corresponding, complementing, equivalent, parallel, analogous

**to have come up with:** to have created, thought up, originated, or conceived

**deep-frying:** cooking

**to dispose of something:** to get rid of or discard something, to clear something out

**used-up:** not being able to make use of again, old

**to enable:** to allow, to entitle, to empower, to make it possible for, to permit

**to put someone in their place:** to humble someone, to take someone down a peg or two

**to have to grapple with something:** to have to struggle with, come to grips with, or deal with something

**stinginess is cool:** thriftiness is in, parsimony is great

**indolence:** inactivity, laziness, sluggishness, idleness

**copy-cat:** imitator, copier

**to open up:** to develop, to build up

**to compare notes:** to exchange, share, or pass on information, to swap opinions

**to take advantage of something:** to make the most of, make use of, or cash in on something

**referral:** reference, recommendation, good word, testimonial

**to approach:** to speak to, to talk to, to make contact with, to get in touch with

**it was a done deal:** everything was accepted, settled, given a positive response, or agreed to

**to bear fruit:** to show results, to pay off, to be successful, to produce results

**to bless:** to provide, to bestow, to endow

*(continúa)*

### Continuación

**line of goods:** range or assortment of goods, product line, line of merchandise

**accessories:** attachments, fixtures, add-ons, extras

**old hand:** veteran, expert, old-timer, master

**to not be able to pull the wool over someone's eyes:** to not be able to fool, trick, deceive, or dupe someone

**to become obvious:** to become clear, apparent, evident, or noticeable

**reusable:** returnable, multi-use

**to tempt:** to allure, to attract, to entice, to persuade, to lure

# *Help customers make more sales*

If sales figures are ***crumbling***, there is only one solution: Help your customers to sell more.

Michael P., who ***attends to*** specialist dealers in the ***sanitary facilities*** industry, really wanted to know why his sales were ***declining***. He started out by comparing his sales ***commission statements*** of the ***past*** four years. The results made him think: *"While the number of customers and orders remained constant, the sales figures per order had been **shrinking** – **on an average of** four to six percent, but with some customers up to 15%."*

## *Precise analysis*

Michael P. now asked himself how to solve this problem. He decided on the following ***approach***: His first step was to inquire among his "shrinking customers" why their order volume was declining constantly. The

results were very ***enlightening*** for him: The majority
of his customers had sales problems of their own,
*"They bought less because they were selling less."*
Some of his customers were increasingly placing
orders with competitors, *"Because they didn't have
much going with their own customers, they tried to
take my customers away from me."*

## Crucial *questions*

After having ***gotten to the bottom of the matter***,
Michael P. began to develop a ***suitable*** strategy. He
had to ask himself some crucial questions first: *"How
can I win back those lost shares in sales?"* and *"How can
I help my customers, who have sales problems of their
own, increase their sales?"*

It was relatively easy for Michael P. to answer the
first question. His customers also bought from
the competition because, ultimately, it was irrelevant
to them from whom they purchased their products,
*"They got pretty much the same and at the same **terms**
from everyone."*

## *Provide* genuine added value

Therefore, the real challenge for Michael P. was
***to afford*** his customers genuine added value which
would make him stand out from the competition. This
additional value, to him, was to make selling easier
for his customers and to support them whenever they
***encountered*** problems in their daily work.

He found the answer while talking to one of his
"shrinking customers." *"I discovered that the way this
customer was going about selling our products would
never work."* So Michael P. saw his mission as giving
his advice and support to his customers for their
sales talks and supplying them with tips and sales
arguments to use with their customers.

# Auxiliary service only where it pays off

Since Michael P.'s strategy initially caused him considerably more work, he had to find an appropriate solution. He decided to provide auxiliary service only to the customers who **are promising**.

Meanwhile, it has become a fascinating challenge for Michael P. to act as sales advisor, *"This has **opened up new vistas** for me because now I'm truly familiar with my customers' world."* Because he had to deal much more intensely with the end customers' world, it **was disclosed to** him by which criteria they think and act when they buy.

The support that Michael P. now **accords to** his customers, made all three worlds come together. By using his company as an example, he shows how a specialist dealer can profit if he **implements** certain management techniques. Michael P. uses other specialist dealers' positive examples in order to describe how end customers can be attended to or how to find interesting niches.

## Palabras para recordar

**to crumble:** to disintegrate, to fall to pieces, to deteriorate, to go down

**to attend to:** to take care of, to give one's attention to, to see to, to focus on

**sanitary facilities:** bathroom fixtures and fittings

**to decline:** to drop, to lessen, to decrease, to diminish, to wane

**commission statement:** percentage receipt, compensation record

**past:** previous, preceding, last

**to shrink:** to get smaller, to reduce, to drop off, to shrivel

*(continúa)*

### *Continuación*

**on an average of:** typically in the region of, more or less around

**approach:** method, procedure, modus operandi

**enlightening:** informative, revealing, helpful, instructive, useful

**crucial:** vital, key, decisive, central

**to get to the bottom of the matter:** to find out the cause or reason for the problem

**suitable:** appropriate, fitting, pertinent

**terms:** conditions, stipulations, specifications, provisions

**genuine:** real, authentic, actual, true, indisputable

**added value:** additional or extra worth

**to afford:** to offer, to give, to provide

**to encounter:** to be faced with, to be confronted with

**auxiliary:** additional, supplementary, extra, secondary, supporting, ancillary, added

**to pay off:** to meet with success, to get results, to be profitable

**to be promising:** to show high potential

**to open up new vistas:** to result in a new perspective or outlook

**to be disclosed to one:** to be revealed, divulged, or unveiled to one

**to accord to:** to give to, to bestow upon, to offer to

**to implement:** to put into practice, to apply, to realise, to employ

# *It pays to be loyal*

Sales representatives act in their own interest when also supporting and ***advising*** customers who find themselves in a difficult business situation. Ideally, they will profit from the ***subsequent recovery*** of that company.

 When business is bad for one of your customers, chances ***decline*** rapidly for the sales force to make a sale. As a result, the sales representatives ***curtail*** their service activities and, instead, concentrate more on those customers whose businesses are doing well.

Initially, this behaviour is certainly understandable and economical, but there can be a ***downside***. And that is the case when the customer has gotten over a difficult phase and from then on ***counts on***

## Special customer problems increase your chances

When a customer comes to you with a special problem, this must not automatically mean a lot more work and effort. Finding a solution together with your customer can result in a long-lasting and trustful collaboration.

Customer problems cannot always be solved ***on the spur of the moment*** and demand quite a bit of energy. Do not leave the customer alone with such a problem, because otherwise he may swiftly drift away to the competition as a result. If a customer confronts you with a problem such as this, you should signal to him that it requires a special solution. Offer your customer to develop a solution together with him. Under no circumstance should you make hasty and ***precipitate*** promises that you cannot keep. Tell him that you need to consult with your colleagues when dealing with unclear issues. Set a specific date for your actions. That way your customer will ***acknowledge*** that you are really ***campaigning*** for him and his ***predicament***.

companies that have really helped him through the
*dire times*.

## Analysis and selection

Therefore, determine which of the customer
companies will probably get back on its course and
which, on the other hand, *are bound to fail*. If the
company is healthy at its *core*, if it has good potential
and if the managers are *capable* enough to master
the crisis, then is pays not to lose one's patience
during the crisis and to *stay true to* the company.

There are *several* different options:

- ✔ You can *pass on* the industry's experience and
  know-how that you have collected during your
  years in the business from other customers
  when they were in a *similar* situation.

- ✔ *Propose* to present your view of the situation to
  the customer in a results-oriented manner.

- ✔ *Confer* with your own company and offer your
  customer *inter-coordinated* terms of payment,
  *grants* for advertising expenses or the like.

Such *measures* can *contribute* in preserving
*promising* customer relationships. It is *decisive*,
however, to signal to the customer that he can count
on his supplier even during hard times. This way,
a customer's crisis can *blossom* into an *enduring*
customer *commitment*.

---

### Palabras para recordar

**to pay:** to be worth one's while or worth it

**to advise:** to give advice to, to counsel, to give an opinion to

**subsequent:** consecutive, successive, following,
succeeding, later

**recovery:** growth, boom, boost, upturn

*(continúa)*

## *Continuación*

**to decline:** to drop, to decrease, to fall

**to curtail:** to limit, to reduce, to shorten

**downside:** disadvantage, harm, drawback, difficulty, snag, snare

**to count on:** to trust in, to believe in

**dire times:** bad, difficult, trying, tough, dismal, dreadful, or critical spell

**to be bound to fail:** to most likely go under, be unsuccessful, or fall short

**core:** foundation, basis, centre, marrow

**capable:** efficient, effective, competent

**to stay true to someone:** to remain loyal, faithful, or dedicated to someone

**several:** a number of, some, a few

**to pass on:** to convey, to communicate

**similar:** alike, comparable, related

**to propose:** to offer, to suggest

**to confer:** to have a consultation, to exchange views, to parley, to deliberate

**inter-coordinated:** aligned, balanced

**grant:** partial funding or allowance, stipend, subvention

**measures:** activities, actions, steps

**to contribute:** to play a role, to be a factor, to play a part

**promising:** encouraging, hopeful

**decisive:** important, crucial, key, pivotal

**to blossom:** to flourish, to thrive, to grow

**enduring:** lasting, continuing, stable

*(continúa)*

---

### *Continuación*

**commitment:** attachment, allegiance

**on the spur of the moment:** at first go, right away, straight away

**precipitate:** hurried, impulsive

**to acknowledge:** to recognise, to appreciate, to admit, to accept

**to campaign:** to work, to stand up, to fight, to champion

**predicament:** problem, challenge, trouble

---

# *Pricing as a* **competitive** *factor*

Aside from product benefit, product pricing is also an effective marketing instrument.

There are businesses, which calculate their products' prices from a cost and *yield* viewpoint. And there are businesses that practise so-called pricing, which means *determining* the prices from a marketing viewpoint and *adjusting* their cost factors and yield targets *accordingly*. An example for *applying* this practise is the machine manufacturer Maho Seebach GmbH, located in Ruhla.

Whenever a new product is created there, the price is also an important development objective: First, the field sales force interviews the customers in order to find out what benefit exactly is needed. Then, research is conducted as to what price the customer is willing to pay for this benefit. Finally, inquiries are made on how the competition is able to fulfil the price/performance requirements in question.

Only after all these important facts are *gathered* can research and development begin.

# Prices need to be customer-oriented

At Maho Seebach, it was discovered that not just a product which does **not comply with** the market's demands can lead to a flop, but also the price can if it is not **assessed** in a consumer oriented way. Then you will hear that well-known sentence from your sales representatives: *"Our product is **far too expensive**. No customer will buy it at that price."*

But if **in the lead-up** it has been clarified which demands the customer is making in regard to product pricing and performance, work is much easier for product developers, purchasing agents, and product managers. They now know which product features the customer **desires** and which **he abstains from**. And they know which quality level is sufficient for the customer. In the second step, the stage is set in the areas of acquisition, manufacturing, and logistics so that the product can be produced at the target price and still **gain** optimal yield.

# Implementing *price adjustments*

The problem, however, is that pricing **is not a constant**, but changes depending on the market situation, as explained by Stephan Kletschke, manager of the Freudenberg Process Seals KG in Viernheim, *"Product innovations can **sustain** their price only over a certain period of time."*

But for this problem there are solutions, according to Björn Schuppar, corporate consultant for Prof. Homburg & Partner in Mannheim. For example, a customer can be bound by providing **auxiliary** services that are **indispensable** to him. **Fearing** complications if he changes suppliers will reduce the customer's sensitivity to the price. So for him, **adhering to** delivery dates, **maintaining** quality standards, or receiving advisory support can be far more financially beneficial than a product's price reduction.

Another method is ***precluding*** a direct price ***comparison*** for the customer. To achieve this, either various products are gathered into a product bundle, for example a machine including a ***spare parts kit***. Or the customer is offered an all-inclusive product/ service package, for example a machine which includes 24-hour customer service.

Typical examples: Together with their Business Partner Innovation Center, IBM Deutschland GmbH supports their small and middle-sized end users in identifying and implementing potential savings in their own companies. Microsoft GmbH in Munich provides their customers with an additional, interactive "trouble-shooting" service. Business customers with more complex inquiries ***are referred to*** a so-called "solutions provider," a goal or product-oriented specialist in a partner company.

## *Alternative distribution channel used as pricing instrument*

Finally, it is possible to take away the customer's economic comparison by choosing an alternative distribution channel. Typical examples are Vorwerk, Avon, and Tupperware-type products that are offered by house-to-house distribution.

Another pricing instrument is the segmentation of customers: Certain customer groups are less sensitive to price than others.

The most important tool for price maintenance, however, is brand management. The more "valuable" the image of a product becomes through ***complementary*** marketing measures, ***the more inclined*** consumers are to pay a certain price. For certain products, it is precisely the high price that increases sales, validating the slogan, *"It has always been a little more expensive **to have good taste**."*

## Palabras para recordar

**competitive:** combative, competition oriented, ready for action

**yield:** earnings, income, returns, profit, proceeds, revenue

**to determine:** to define, to establish, to fix, to constitute, to decide

**to adjust:** to adapt, to fine-tune, to align, to arrange, to orientate

**accordingly:** appropriately, correspondingly, properly, suitably

**to apply:** to use, to put to use, to employ, to utilise

**to gather:** to compile, to bring together, to round up, to put together

**to not comply with:** to not fulfil, follow, obey, conform to, or adhere to

**to assess:** to define, to determine, to establish, to consider

**far too expensive:** much too, by a great amount too, or markedly too costly

**in the lead-up:** prior, earlier, in advance

**to desire:** to want, to need, to fancy, to be bent on

**to abstain from:** to refrain from, to renounce, to do without, to forbear

**to gain:** to achieve, to arrive at, to pick up, to build up, to secure

**to implement:** to put into effect, to realise, to carry out, to execute

**to not be a constant:** to not be a steady factor, an absolute term, or an invariable

**to sustain:** to hold, to maintain, to uphold, to preserve

**auxiliary:** additional, supplementary, extra, secondary, supporting, ancillary, added

*(continúa)*

### *Continuación*

**indispensable:** essential, necessary, high-priority, fundamental, key

**to fear:** to be afraid of, to worry about, to be anxious about, to be scared of

**to adhere to:** to stick to, to hold to, to fulfil, to be faithful to

**to maintain:** to uphold, to keep up, to preserve, to keep in existence

**to preclude:** to prevent, to prohibit, to make impossible, to rule out, to bar

**comparison:** contrast, differentiation, collation, judgement, evaluation

**spare parts kit:** extra, additional, or reserve set of components

**are referred to:** are directed, forwarded, sent, or transferred to

**complementary:** accompanying, supplementary

**the more inclined:** the more willing, ready, predisposed, prone, or liable

**to have good taste:** to have style, elegance, stylishness, or finesse

# *Less is more* – selective use *of* handouts

*As a matter of principle,* it makes sense *to adhere to* the motto "less is more," because when you give a customer *more handouts than what he can put up with*, he will just *tune out*. You should consider this when you use brochures, demo CDs or the like. Very closely watch his reaction and spontaneously decide whether you will keep sending new informational material his way.

*To what extent* you *utilise* these respective media samples *depends on* your customer's preferences: Some people need to hold something in their hand. They print out everything, carefully work through brochures, mark important passages, and *annotate* them with post-its. *Crucial* to this is always the quality of the dialogue: Take into account that the presentation should not end up as a monologue.

## Palabras para recordar

**selective use:** targeted, purposeful, discerning, or careful usage

**as a matter of principle:** basically, on principle

**to adhere to:** to stick to, to hold fast to, to comply with, to be faithful to, to follow

**more than what one can put up with:** more than what one can endure, bear, or tolerate

**to tune out:** to turn away from it all, to stop paying attention

**to what extent:** to what degree, amount, level, or point

**to utilise:** to make use of, to employ, to resort to, to take advantage of

**to depend on:** to be contingent upon, subject to, based upon, or influenced by

**to annotate:** to comment on, to add notes to, to add footnotes to

**crucial:** decisive, pivotal, essential, vital, necessary, critical

# Paving the way for *the sale*

Promotional material is effective if it *is attuned to* the potential customer's information needs. When running advertising campaigns, it is *common practice* in many companies to send prospectuses, brochures, catalogues and other promotional material to potential customers. Thomas Burzler, chief executive officer of sales motion in Dillingen/Donau, however, *advises against* such practice.

He recommends that the internal sales force call the potential customer beforehand in order to determine what his *current* requirements are and what type of information he is most interested in. *"Otherwise it would be pure luck if a prospect happened to be genuinely interested and considered purchasing at that time,"* says Thomas Burzler. *"The more common scenario is that the prospect is not even aware of a need or problem."* In this case, it would not work to send detailed promotional material about products and solutions to the potential customer because he will be neither interested nor willing to study the brochures. *"However, it is a good idea to send out more general information leaflets once in a while to keep the prospect reminded of you,"* explains Thomas Burzler. *"These leaflets should not be too detailed but still give the potential customer a good idea about the products you offer or the services you render, in case of need."*

## How often to contact the prospect?

The right number of contacts is the deciding factor when it comes to making the prospective customer think immediately about your company at the right moment. Thomas Burzler recommends doubling the time between each contact. For example: Immediately after the telephone call, send initial information about your company to the prospect. He will receive it in about two days. You may call him about four days later, **referring to** the information you sent him. One week later, an e-mail newsletter could be the next contact, etc. If the contact frequency is at about four to six months, which passes very quickly, this frequency may **be maintained**. *"Newsletters and similar promotional* **aids** *are very appropriate in this case,"* says Thomas Burzler.

## If there is concrete interest

If there is specific interest on the prospect's part, it **is advantageous** to send him individualised information, **tailored to** his requirements.

You should save him the trouble of having to leaf through an **entire** catalogue. *"For example, you could use post-it notes with hand-written tips to guide him to the information that interests him most,"* suggests Thomas Burzler. He also recommends making specific reference to the **previous** phone call in the **cover letter**. Instead of writing, *"Per our phone conversation, enclosed please find the information you requested,"* the **recipient** will pay more attention to the promotional material if he finds special tips and explanations in the text of the cover letter, saying *"You were especially interested in our solution for… Please find details on page… I've* **highlighted** *the important* **paragraphs** *in the brochure for you."*

## Be careful with requests for written offers

If someone asks for a written offer or to receive promotional material, Burzler also recommends calling the prospect first. *"One may* **safely assume** *that the prospect also requests information from competitors and compares it, purely on price, if he doesn't have other criteria to go by."*

Calling the prospect to determine the actual requirements gives the internal sales force the opportunity *to distinguish themselves from* other competitors, should they only send out written material. *"Besides, over the phone you can find out what it's all about and which problem the prospect needs a solution for. With this knowledge in hand, you are able to customise the written information to the potential customer's requirements and wishes,"* says Burzler. *"Consequently, this will **increase** the chances for success."*

---

## Palabras para recordar

**to pave the way for something:** to prepare, clear the way, or make preparations for something

**to be attuned to:** to be adjusted, tailored, fitted, or assimilated to

**common practice:** customary, everyday, routine, or standard procedure

**to advise against something:** to warn or caution not to do something

**current:** present, present-day, existing, ongoing

**to be pure luck:** to be good fortune, a sheer blessing, or an utter stoke of luck

**to be genuinely interested:** to be truly or really intrigued

**to not be aware of something:** to not be conscious or in the know about something

**leaflet:** booklet, brochure, pamphlet, flier

**to render:** to provide, to give, to deliver, to supply, to make available

**to refer to:** to mention, to bring up, to talk about, to speak of

**to be maintained:** to be kept up, continued, kept going, or carried on

**aids:** means, tools, resources

*(continúa)*

### *Continuación*

**to be advantageous:** to be beneficial, helpful, useful, or of benefit

**tailored to:** modified to, adapted to, adjusted to, customised to

**entire:** whole, complete, full

**previous:** earlier, preceding, prior

**cover letter:** first page of the written message

**recipient:** receiver, addressee

**to highlight:** to mark, to tag

**paragraph:** section, part, item

**to safely assume something:** to take something for granted, to surely expect something

**to distinguish oneself from:** to set oneself apart from, to single oneself out from

**to increase:** to add to, to boost, to augment, to enhance, to heighten

# Approaching *customers* on the spot

With the help of geo-marketing, target areas and available addresses can be examined for their potential *in advance*. This regionally individualised target group approach is the key to success in direct marketing.

In the geo-strategic optimising of a direct marketing campaign, not only demographic data such as age, profession, household income, or information pertaining to product *affinity* play a part, but also the *proximity* to the competition, or the distance and

routes to the supplier's locations and branch offices.

The available amount of data on business and consumer target audiences is enormous: Schober's *subsidiary*, Infas Geodaten, has a household database including 35 million home addresses *at their disposal*, selectable by microgeographic characteristics, more than five million so-called lifestyle addresses, selectable according to specific buying intentions, consumer *focal points* and interests, more than seven million private email addresses with *consent* for email marketing, and more than five million business addresses in Germany, Austria, and Switzerland.

With the help of geo-information systems, the GfK (Association for Consumer Research) Geomarketing is optimising their customers' dialogue marketing campaigns. In this process, *applicable* addresses are filtered from the existing pool of addresses, responses are analysed, and the levels of efficiency are compared. What lies behind this: In a mailing campaign, the response rate can *indeed* be measured but most of the time the senders *are deprived of* the information about where exactly their informative letters had a high response and in which regions a comparatively small response was achieved.

By using a *recent* example, the mechanism of the geo-strategic optimising process becomes clear: Mailings were to be sent to retail businesses. The following objectives *were to be taken into account*: To localise profitable target areas and target groups in order to minimise or altogether avoid *wastage*, to measure the mailings' response rate differentiated according to regions, and to determine its consequences for sales. The goal was to reach retail businesses that are located in *affluent* regions allowing the sender of the informative letters to achieve a high contribution margin.

*Initially*, for the selection and evaluation of this data, the addresses were important. On the basis of the *postal code*, they were put into a geographical order and placed on a *map*. Because of the addresses' geographic relation, more potential factors *could be taken into consideration*. For example: What part of the general buying power is available for the retail industry? Through this procedure, it was possible to find locations with strong retail trade – and these regions were especially interesting for the mailing campaign.

The costs for geo-strategic optimising of direct marketing campaigns vary, *dependent on* the depth of the analytical examination. If a client simply wants to isolate regions according to one specific characteristic like buying power, a few hundred Euros will *suffice*. For a more precise approach – perhaps down to the geocoordinate level and that for many regions – the expenses could possibly reach the six-figure area.

In order *to raise* the economic efficiency of geo-marketing, let your company's various departments such as marketing, media planning and sales, share the secured data.

## Palabras para recordar

**to approach:** to make advances to, to make a proposal to, to proposition

**on the spot:** on the scene, locally, on location, on site

**in advance:** beforehand, prior, ahead of time, earlier

**affinity:** partiality, attraction, liking, inclination

**proximity:** nearness, adjacency, vicinity, propinquity, closeness

**subsidiary:** affiliate, associated company, daughter company

**to have at one's disposal:** to have available or on hand

*(continúa)*

### *Continuación*

**focal point:** focus, emphasis, main focus, main area of concern

**consent:** permission, go-ahead, authority, agreement, sanction

**applicable:** relevant, appropriate, pertinent, valid

**indeed:** in fact, rightly, actually, positively, for sure

**to be deprived of:** to be denied, to lack, to be deficient of, to be left without

**recent:** current, new, fresh, topical

**were to be taken into account:** were to be considered, included, regarded, or taken into consideration

**wastage:** deviation from spreading or distribution

**affluent:** wealthy, well-to-do, well off, moneyed

**initially:** first of all, at first, in the first instance

**postal code:** zip code, post code

**map:** chart, plan

**could be taken into consideration:** could be included, regarded, kept in mind, or incorporated

**dependent on:** conditional on, contingent on, determined by, subject to

**to suffice:** to be adequate, sufficient, or enough

**to raise:** to advance, to augment, to elevate, to heighten, to improve

# In-depth *knowledge about sales* territories

Only if the sales manager has all relevant information on his desk, is he able to make goal-oriented decisions for his sales territories

*"**If you want to last in business**, you have to be flexible and this requires getting all relevant market and customer information from each sales territory **at any given time**,"* is how Franz-Xaver Frischhut, **head of accounting** at Hamberger Industriewerke GmbH, Stephanskirchen, explains one of his company's most important decisions: The manufacturer of parquet floors **set up** an IT-supported sales controlling system.

According to Frischhut, in order to be able to act quickly, one needs **reliable**, extensive data **without delay**, *"Not just general figures are important, but also detailed analyses, **broken down into** individual product and customer groups per sales territory."* Above all, controlling of the sales territories is, in itself, an important leadership tool for the in-house sales managers: *"The more up-to-date and precise the information they're getting is, **the more confident** they can lead their sales force."*

## Overview at the push of a button

After the project's completion, the benefits **become apparent**: The approximately 30 users from management, sales, and accounting receive all information at the push of a button, which before they were able to determine only after doing **elaborate** research: **Planned/actual comparisons** of sales and results classified by customers, products, and branch sales offices.

By feeding not just the company's internal information but also market research data into the data base, the sales managers get an idea about which territories *still need to be developed* or where market shares can *be wrested* from competitors. *"And what's all-important: One also finds out where you can push through which prices,"* says Franz-Xaver Frischhut.

---

## Palabras para recordar

**in-depth:** thorough, detailed, comprehensive, extensive, profound

**territory:** area, section, route

**if you want to last in business:** if you desire to continue, carry on, remain, or keep on in commerce

**at any given time:** at all times, all the time, each time, every time

**head of accounting:** chief, director, manager, or person in charge of bookkeeping

**to set up:** to establish, to start, to institute, to bring into being, to initiate

**reliable:** dependable, trustworthy, well-founded, credible, sound

**without delay:** quickly, fast, immediately, promptly, expeditiously

**broken down into:** separated, categorised, classified, or itemised into

**the more confident:** the more sure, positive, convinced, or secure

**overview at the push of a button:** overall view or general idea at a mouse click

**to become apparent:** to become clear, evident, obvious, discernible, or noticeable

**elaborate:** complicated, detailed, complex, painstaking, careful

*(continúa)*

### *Continuación*

**planned/actual comparison:** contrast of intended and confirmed data

**still need to be developed:** yet require to be tapped or opened up

**to be wrested:** to be wrung, taken away, or removed

**to push through:** to get through, to get accepted

# *SUV* heats up *business with new customers*

During the pre-launch campaign for the Porsche Cayenne, existing and *prospective customers*, as well as *dealers* and their staff, were intensely and successfully prepared for the arrival of the new car model by the automobile manufacturer from Stuttgart.

For decades, Porsche has been *the epitome of* sports cars. However, with the *introduction* of the Cayenne model, a five-door, *all-terrain* sports utility vehicle (SUV), the Swabian car builder *entered unknown territory*. The company strategists and the trade partners were confronted with new tasks *in regard to* customer segmentation and sales approach. In their research, the Porsche marketers determined that a Cayenne's potential buyer *hardly differs* from the *owner* of a classic Porsche sports car. The social background, above all, turned out to be nearly identical.

From their in-house market research, Porsche also knew that drivers of the 911 and Boxster models typically own two additional vehicles, one of them often being an SUV or a luxury limousine.

Therefore, *it could be assumed* that within this target group, which already shows a high degree of Porsche affinity, a strong interest for a sporty Porsche SUV would exist. *"There was a high possibility* *that the Cayenne would sooner or later **replace** our existing customers' different brand limousines or SUVs,"* explains a Porsche marketer. *"And because we have relatively good knowledge of our existing customers, we were able **to address** them directly and successfully."*

The second core target group for the Cayenne identified by the Porsche marketers were owners of SUVs and limousines of other brands who find the brand Porsche attractive and ***appealing***. They perhaps have a certain affinity toward the 911 or Boxster but for family or other reasons so far have ***refrained from*** purchasing a classic sports car and therefore have not become a customer.

During the one-year pre-launch campaign, drivers of the models 911 and Boxster and new prospects were informed ***continually*** about the Cayenne's product details. New customer addresses were acquired by means of an integrated communications strategy. This strategy ***comprised*** all elements of the marketing mix – from the classic advertisement with response elements to ***measures*** at the dealerships, dialogue marketing activities, for example a sixstep mailing campaign, to using the internet as information medium and the active acquisition of prospects. At the end of the pre-launch campaign, Porsche had acquired 25 000 addresses of prospective customers in Germany alone. 54 000 visitors came to the nationwide events at the Porsche centres on the occasion of the Cayenne's sales promotion ***to inspect*** the SUV personally.

In order to bind the newly acquired customers long-term to the Porsche brand and the respective dealership "Porsche Centre"), the company supplied its trade partners with an entire package of customer-***retention*** programmes.

Among them are safety training and sports car driving-days on ***blocked off*** race tracks, the Porsche sports driving school, the customer magazine *Christophorus*, or the customer newspaper *Porsche Times*, ***tailored to*** each Porsche Centre and its respective offer. In addition, the dealers regularly send personal notes to their customers and they are offered a ***membership*** in their local Porsche Club. These customer clubs are *registered associations* and are *largely* independent of the Porsche Company but still receive its *tremendous* care and support.

Conclusion: Porsche's sales approach for the Cayenne's pre-launch campaign *proved to be* a complete success: With a total of 15 299 newly registered vehicles in Germany, Porsche *set up* a registration record in the *fiscal* year 2003/2004. More than one third, 5872 of them, were Cayenne automobiles.

---

## Palabras para recordar

**to heat up:** to boost, to increase, to expand, to develop, to amplify

**prospective customer:** potential, future, likely, or soon-to-be client

**dealer:** trader, wholesaler

**the epitome of:** the essence, quintessence, embodiment, or archetype of

**introduction:** launch, presentation, promotion

**all-terrain:** cross-country

**to enter unknown territory:** to go into an unfamiliar or unexplored area

**in regard to:** on the subject of, as to, concerning, on the matter of

**to hardly differ:** to barely be different or dissimilar

**owner:** possessor, holder, keeper

**it could be assumed:** it could be taken for granted, presupposed, presumed, or believed

**to replace:** to take the place of, to supersede, to succeed, to come after

**to address:** to reach, to contact, to get in touch with, to get a message to

*(continúa)*

## *Continuación*

**appealing:** likeable, pleasing, interesting, engaging

**to refrain from:** to do without, to hold back, to forgo, to avoid

**continually:** repeatedly, frequently, regularly, constantly

**to comprise:** to include, to consist of, to contain, to be composed of

**measures:** course of action, steps, proceedings

**to inspect:** to take a close look at, to examine, to check out

**retention:** preservation, maintenance, loyalty

**blocked off:** closed off, cordoned off, barricaded, fenced off

**tailored to:** customised for, designed for, adapted to, modified for

**membership:** participation, involvement

**registered association:** registered as recorded club, society, organisation, or group

**largely:** for the most part, basically, to a large extent, to a great degree

**tremendous:** great, enormous, immense

**to prove to be:** to turn out to be, to end up being, to emerge as, to become

**to set up:** to establish, to produce, to achieve, to pull off

**fiscal:** business, financial, economic

# Capítulo 4

# Atender al cliente y tratar con él

* * * * * * * * * * * * * * * * * * * * * * *

### En este capítulo

▶ Cómo mantener clientes

▶ Cómo retomar el contacto con antiguos clientes

▶ Cómo recuperar a clientes perdidos

▶ Qué podemos aprender del cliente

* * * * * * * * * * * * * * * * * * * * * * *

*H*asta ahora hemos visto que para vender un producto hay que saber hablar. No obstante, solemos olvidarnos de un proceso de capital importancia: también hay que saber escuchar al cliente. El trato diario con los clientes puede ser una magnífica oportunidad de negocio, pero también de crecimiento personal. Cerrar una venta puede ser fácil: lo difícil es conseguir que se repita. La humildad, la capacidad de escuchar y la permeabilidad a buenas ideas pueden ser claves para mantener clientes, retomar un contacto después de mucho tiempo, o incluso recuperar a un cliente a quien se perdió por motivos que debes aprender a interpretar.

No podemos enseñarte a leerles la mente a tus clientes, pero sí a escuchar sus quejas, a establecer con ellos unos lazos de sinceridad y confianza y, en última instancia, a aprender de ellos. Todo esto te ayudará a aumentar las ventas, sí, pero también será una valiosa fuente de ideas.

# Long-term retention *of age 50+* customers

The tour operator TUI Germany *has a knack* for winning and retaining the frequently travelling and *generously spending* group of over 50 year-olds by providing *customised* offers.

For travel businesses, 50+ customers are an important and *sought-after* target group. These customers *expect a great deal* but are also willing *to dig deep into their pockets* to finance their vacation travels. But the 50+ target group is very heterogeneous, *"For today's over 50 year-olds, age itself doesn't mean that much anymore ,"* explains Andreas Casdorff, head of product Line Management and Development for TUI Germany, *"because these peoples' self-image has changed a lot."* Characters and life situations of people aged 50+ *are quite varied*. Some are still working, while others *are* already *retired*. Frequently, people who just *crossed the 50s threshold* still have their children living with them, while older representatives of this target group are already grandparents. *"From these criteria, quite different vacation needs arise,"* explains Casdorff – and these different parameters have consequences for the *sales approach*.

That is why the tour operator first analysed the following questions, *independently from* the age issue: What is the target group's motive for a vacation? What do these people expect from a vacation? What do they want to experience while on vacation? What are their value orientations?

The over 50 group's younger representatives still show a presence in almost all the TUI product segments. They book relaxation and wellness offers just as often as activity vacations. However, there is a clear *distinction* between customers over 60 and the younger representatives of the target group, *"As the 60+ customers don't have to go to work anymore, their social environment may have become noticeably restricted,"* Casdorff **elucidates**, *"so when this target group takes a vacation, the concept of community takes on a more important role."* The TUI product Club Elan **caters precisely to** these needs. Club Elan is the centre point for the older customers, the **creation** of a community, and stands in the foreground of all activities.

The community aspect in turn **contributes to** the acquisition of new customers, especially among the 50+ **crowd**. Older people, especially, talk a lot about their vacation experiences. So there is a relatively high probability that a satisfied customer will bring in a new one.

Club Elan is one of the most actively **pursued** products in TUI's customer relationship management. *"Direct communication with the target group is an important subject,"* says Andreas Casdorff, *"and that is why we designed a website for Club Elan, where customers are able to communicate either with TUI or with each other."* With support of the Club Elan website, which, according to Casdorff, is used enthusiastically by the older customers, TUI is keeping its customer relationships going year-round and is keeping the brand in the customers' **consciousness**. Another factor contributing to success is Club Elan's own customer magazine, which is sent to customers several times per year with the idea of **tying them to** the brand. *"This medium, too, meets this target group's high demand for communication. The customer magazine offers customers the chance to publish their own articles, such as travel reports. That way the target group **remains** involved in the brand world because it **regards** this TUI medium, the one it co-designs, as its own,"* says Casdorff.

Conclusion: Differentiating their sales approach according to the **various** vacation needs of the 50 and over customers pays off for TUI.

The customised offers for older travellers produce growth rates of over 20 %. Customer loyalty is enormous. 83 % of all Club Elan customers have booked this offer at least twice before.

With travel operator brands such as TUI, Dr. Tigges, Airtours, 1-2-Fly, L'Tur, or Wolters Reisen, TUI Deutschland GmbH is the leading travel and *leisure time* business in Germany and a 100 % daughter of the TUI AG. In the fiscal year 2004, its 58 000 employees made 18 billion Euros in sales.

## Palabras para recordar

**long-term retention:** lasting preservation, longstanding maintenance

**to have a knack for something:** to have a skill, talent, flair, or a special ability for something

**generously spending:** liberally splurging or consuming

**customised:** tailored, personalised, custom-made, modified

**sought-after:** very popular, very much in demand

**to expect a great deal:** to make great demands, to be more demanding

**to dig deep into one's pockets:** to spend a lot of money

**to be quite varied:** to be very diverse, different, or unlike

**to be retired:** to have given up work, to have stopped working, to be pensioned off

**to cross the 50s threshold:** to turn 50, to celebrate one's 50th birthday

**to arise:** to surface, to develop, to crop up, to appear, to evolve

**sales approach:** selling strategy or tactic

**independently from:** separately from, unrelated to, detached from

*(continúa)*

### *Continuación*

**distinction:** difference, dissimilarity, division, contrast

**environment:** situation, surroundings, setting, milieu

**noticeably restricted:** distinctly or markedly limited

**to elucidate:** to explain, to make clear, to clarify, to reveal

**to cater precisely to:** to meet, to fulfil, to comply with, to fit

**creation:** formation, making, establishment, construction

**to contribute to:** to be a factor in, to play a part in, to play a role in

**crowd:** group, set, circle, clique

**pursued:** chased, worked at, aimed at, engaged in

**consciousness:** mind, thoughts, awareness, memory, cognizance

**to tie someone to:** to bind someone to, to make someone stay loyal to

**to remain:** to stay, to keep on being, to continue to be

**to regard:** to look upon, to view, to see

**various:** different, diverse, assorted, miscellaneous, choice of

**leisure time:** free time, spare time, time off

# *Reactivating jeopardised customer relations*

***Reinforce*** the "strategic ***points of intersection***" to meet your customer.

Your sales representative's ***lack of*** emotional ***immediacy*** toward the customer may be interpreted as impoliteness and his ***credibility*** may be lacking as a result of carelessness, especially when promises were not delivered reliably, and his inflexibility may possibly be perceived as lacking in creativity. The customer relationship *appears to be "muddled"*.

But what is there to do? Better to play it safe from the start: Take the line of demarcation between your sales organisation and the customer as the starting point, where *frictionless* interactions *are supposed to connect*. And occupy this *pivotal point* not just with one single sales representative, who is only in touch with one single customer. Because you know: *a bird can never fly with one wing.*

For the most part, it is better to have a complete sales team in the supplier's company to communicate on various levels with the buyer's organisation.

Establish "strategic points of intersection":

- ✔ Where do the customer's strengths and weaknesses come into view? Are they *in accord with* your own company's?

- ✔ Which key personalities in the customer organisation are crucial for the success *of endeavouring towards* a more solid commitment? Who are the supporters and who is a potential saboteur?

- ✔ Who is a high-ranking decision maker in the buyer's organisation, one who supports the principle of "customer intimacy" and supplies the necessary *backing*?

This is not supposed to mean that the connection simply stands and falls with one such person. There can be others, depending on the size of the customer's company. Please note: Companies with experience in regard to "customer intimacy" are looking to connect to the right teams in the customer organisation straight from the beginning. This will not only provide the required working environment, but also signals **the purest of intentions**.

As soon as a person has taken up a specific position, a constructive and consistent stream of communication needs **to commence** to cement the ties. Constantly verify whether the demands are being met! Despite the **phrase-mongering** in many brochures – inspire in your customer **the heartfelt notion that he actually does take centre stage!**

## *Secure lasting success*

Please never forget: In this philosophy, sales revenues initially are not identical to success. Success will **ensue** when the customer runs a project with you that has clearly contributed to their **advancement**. Yet, this **imperatively** means that all parties involved need to have an understanding and acceptance what exactly this advancement consists of.

Or approach your customer, should they at some point **bemoan** profit collapses, and offer **to amend** their contracts in a flexible manner. In the long run, such small concessions contribute, for example, to the **fortification of trust**, when difficulties are experienced and **endured** together.

---

## Palabras para recordar

**jeopardised:** threatened, imperilled, vulnerable

**to reinforce:** to strengthen, to fortify, to give a boost to, to bolster

**point of intersection:** meeting or crossing point, juncture, node

**lack of:** absence, deprivation, or shortage of

**immediacy:** nearness, closeness, propinquity

*(continúa)*

## *Continuación*

**credibility:** trustworthiness, reliability, integrity, authority, standing

**appears to be muddled:** seems to be messed up, tangled, or in shambles

**frictionless:** smooth, unobstructed, trouble-free

**are supposed to connect:** should link up with one another

**pivotal point:** central point, focal point

**a bird can never fly with one wing:** you cannot stand while having only one foot on the ground

**in accord with:** in concurrence, agreement, or accordance with

**of endeavouring towards:** of striving for, of trying one's hand at, of attempting, of making an effort for

**backing:** support, help, assistance, encouragement, cooperation

**the purest of intentions:** honourable, upright, or decent objectives

**to commence:** to begin, to start

**phrase-mongering:** hot air, waffling, flannelling, gobbledygook

**the heartfelt notion:** the sincere, genuine, profound, or deep belief

**that he actually does take centre stage:** that he is really the focus of attention or interest

**to ensue:** to develop, to follow, to occur, to happen, to turn up, to transpire

**advancement:** progress, improvement, development, furtherance

**imperatively:** coercively, stringently, strictly, rigorously

**to bemoan:** to complain, moan, or grumble about

*(continúa)*

---

### Continuación

**to amend:** to make changes to, to alter, to make corrections to, to modify

**fortification of trust:** strengthening or reinforcement of confidence

**to endure:** to weather, to withstand, to stick out, to get through

---

# Special Report: How to recapture lost customers

## Customer, come back!

In her newly published book *Come back! How to recapture lost customers* Anne Schüller shows the five steps to recapturing lost customers quickly and successfully. The book also ***devotes*** a section to the prevention of customer loss.

## The start

Customer revitalisation management starts where all ***retention measures have failed***, which means that the customer has officially ***terminated*** the business relationship or ***left tacitly***. According to loyalty marketing expert Anne Schüller, two aspects ***arise from this***:

- ✔ Cancellation management: the ***objective*** is ***to ward off*** cancellations or induce customers ***to withdraw them***.

- ✔ Revitalisation management: the objective is ***to resume*** business relationships which had ***discontinued*** or had ***fizzled out***.

It ***is crucial*** to find out immediately which customer left, for what reasons and how to go about recapturing that customer in order to do better *the second time around*. Schüller presents the customer revitalisation management in five steps:

1. Identification of the lost or "sleeping" customers.

2. Analysis of the reasons for loss.

3. Planning and *implementation* of regaining measures.

4. Result checking and optimisation.

5. Prevention.

## Find out the true reasons

The author points out that the true reasons for losing a customer are often emotional ones. Rarely is customer loss a matter of price. "Too expensive" is a wonderful *pretext* for both sides: It's an easy way out for the customer because he doesn't have to give any reasons and is not pushed *to disclose* his "emotional *pain*," as Schüller describes it. For his counterpart on the selling side, it *is convenient* because it allows him *to evade* taking personal responsibility. However, if you don't know the real reasons you are not able to plan and implement corrective measures.

To be successful, it is critical to be aware of customers' *expectations*; customers, who just left, are very helpful in pointing out your company's *strengths and weaknesses*. It is important to pay close attention to the *cancellation notices* and to keep an eye on the *complaint* statistics. Of course, your company should also *conduct* customer *surveys* on a regular basis.

Anne Schüller's practical tips for conducting a customer survey:

✔ Which goals are to be achieved by conducting the survey?

✔ What exactly do you want to know from the lost customers?

✔ Which customers are to be asked? – Do you ask them for their *permission* to do the survey so they don't feel like you *throw them a curve?*

✔ Which survey method is suitable? Who will conduct it? Has it been *ensured* that this method brings relevant results?

✔ How will the results be *processed*, interpreted and presented? Who will receive them?

✔ Who *is in charge of* making the necessary action plans? Who implements them? Who controls them?

✔ How do customers find out about the improvement processes?

## *Hard and soft*

There are *obvious* and *measurable* complaints, which are the "hard" facts, such as:

✔ wrong or missing information waiting periods are too long (telephone, etc.),

✔ delivery or installation periods are too long,

✔ *lacking adherence to delivery dates*,

✔ poor or *deteriorating* product or service, quality,

✔ *breach of agreements,*

✔ *errors in invoicing*, etc.

According to Schüller, the soft factors *are intangible* and much more *connected with* the customers' expectations.

The following soft factors may lead to losing customers:

✔ not enough contact; the customer feels he's been forgotten,

✔ the contacts' *impolite* and unfriendly behaviour,

✔ lack of ***responsiveness*** to and interest in the customers' needs,

✔ not enough flexibility (possibly because of administrative structures),

✔ ***discord*** between salesperson and customer or frequent change of contacts,

✔ poor complaint management, etc. After the analysis, recapturing measures need to be finalised quickly.

✔ Which customer is to be recaptured?

✔ Who is ***to approach*** the lost customers?

✔ What do we offer them?

✔ When will that happen?

✔ How much of the budget ***is available*** for this?

✔ What is the concrete course of action?

In the next step, customers are segmented into profitable and unprofitable ones. After a great deal of ***preparatory work***, measures have to be scheduled – in Schüller's view, communication is the central ***tool*** for approaching lost customers. She ***rates*** verbal communication much higher than the written one. Following, the success hierarchy:

✔ personal conversation,

✔ telephone conversation,

✔ letter, offer, mailing,

✔ e-mail, text message. After the measures have been finalised, the results and success rates are to be determined.

## Palabras para recordar

**to recapture:** to bring back, to return with, to go and get, to get hold of, to win back, to regain, to recover, to reclaim

**to devote:** to assign, to allot, to set aside, to offer, to dedicate

**retention measures:** preservation or maintenance actions

*(continúa)*

## *Continuación*

**to have failed:** to have been unsuccessful, fallen through, or not succeeded

**to terminate:** to end, to stop

**to leave tacitly:** to go away quietly, to depart without saying a word

**to arise from this:** to appear, surface, evolve, or emerge from this

**objective:** goal, intention, purpose

**to ward off:** to fend off, to beat off, to stave off, to avert, to rule out, to repel, to repulse, to keep at bay, to fight off

**to withdraw something:** to take something back, to retract something

**to resume:** to start again, to recommence, to restart, to take up again

**to discontinue:** to stop, to come to a halt, to be terminated or broken off

**to fizzle out:** to peter out, to fold, to flop, to fall through

**to be crucial:** to be critical, essential, important, or key

**the second time around:** at the next try or attempt

**implementation:** execution, carrying out, enforcement

**pretext:** excuse, alleged reason, pretence, cover

**to disclose:** to reveal, to make known, to divulge, to impart

**pain:** hurting, suffering, unhappiness

**to be convenient:** to be opportune, useful, or favourable

**to evade:** to avoid, to dodge, to shake off, to sidestep

**expectations:** outlook, viewpoint

**strengths and weaknesses:** good and bad points, positive and negative sides

*(continúa)*

## *Continuación*

**cancellation notice:** letter of annulment, termination, or cessation

**complaint:** criticism, grievance, statement of dissatisfaction

**to conduct:** to carry out, to do

**survey:** opinion poll, review, analysis

**permission:** consent, authorisation, go-ahead, agreement, okay, say-so

**to throw someone a curve:** to take someone unawares, to throw someone off their guard

**ensured:** made sure, made certain, guaranteed, warranted

**processed:** sorted out, handled,

**to be in charge of something:** to be responsible or accountable for something

**obvious:** clear, palpable, noticeable, visible, discernible, recognisable

**measurable:** assessable, estimable, appraisable, fathomable

**lacking adherence to delivery dates:** failing to distribute merchandise on time or punctually

**deteriorating:** worsening, declining, going downhill, weakening

**breach of agreements:** breaking, violating, or contravention of contracts

**error in invoicing:** mistake, inaccuracy, or miscalculation in billing

**to be intangible:** to be impalpable or untouchable

**connected with:** linked to, associated with, related to

**impolite:** rude, ill-mannered, bad-mannered, discourteous, ungracious

*(continúa)*

### *Continuación*

**responsiveness:** receptiveness, sensitivity, openness, reaction

**discord:** friction, disagreement, difference of opinion, dissension, conflict

**to approach:** to speak to, to talk to, to get in touch with, to make contact with

**is available:** is to be had, is on hand, is obtainable, is existing

**preparatory work:** preliminary, introductory, or basic effort

**tool:** instrument, resource, vehicle, catalyst, channel

**to rate:** to regard, to esteem, to value

# *The customer as ideas provider*

Salespeople, who are proactive in getting **suggestions for improvement** from their customers, **strengthen** the customer relationship and provide useful impulses to their company.

When Mark D., a sales representative for a plastics producer, takes **samples** along to his customers they know that they are "**faced with a challenge**" because the sales representative **is not content** with **polite** answers. *"I want to know exactly what the customer's opinion is, what **bothers** him about the material, and what he would like to be different."*

To him, direct and honest answers are the only useful responses, *"Once a customer **became annoyed** and explained to me that I **didn't need to bother** to come back with such a product and why. I was even glad to get this reaction because I **pass on** honest customer feedback to my sales manager and the research and development department. This kind of feedback* *provides us with important **clues** as to what our customers really need."*

The ***aforementioned*** customer was very surprised when Mark D. invited him, just like that, to the next customer workshop, *"In our company, ideas workshops with customers take place on a regular basis, first to get to know them better and then to be proactive in obtaining their suggestions for improvement. Basically, each suggestion for improvement made by a customer is an important impulse for us."*

In addition to these product-oriented suggestions for improvement, customers are asked regularly whether they are satisfied with the way the sales representatives look after them. *"In this case also, I **prefer** an honest feedback over a polite one,"* says Mark D. *"After all I don't visit them just **to pass the time**. I want my visits to be profitable for both sides."*

---

## Palabras para recordar

**provider:** supplier, source, contributor, bringer, giver

**suggestion for improvement:** proposal, proposition, or plan for betterment

**to strengthen:** to make stronger, to give strength to, to fortify, to give a boost to

**sample:** example, model, representative type

**to be faced with a challenge:** to be confronted with a difficult task

**to not be content:** to not be satisfied, pleased, or comfortable

**polite:** diplomatic, polished, tactful, subtle, suave

**to bother:** to worry, to trouble, to concern, to distress

**to become annoyed:** to become angry, irritated, exasperated, or upset

*(continúa)*

---

### *Continuación*

**to not need to bother:** to not need to concern oneself, to not take the time or effort

---

**to pass on:** to convey, to forward, to impart, to communicate

---

**clue:** information, sign, hint, evidence, pointer

---

**aforementioned:** previously described, forenamed, abovementioned

---

**to prefer:** to favour, to choose, to select, to pick

---

**to pass the time:** to while away, occupy, or spend the hours

---

# Complaints *are opportunities*

Sales representatives need to take each customer complaint seriously and **respond** immediately.

Many times Wolf T., a sales representative for a supplier in Essen, has received text messages like this one from his colleagues in the internal sales force, *"Call customer XYZ right away, he's very* **upset***!"* – *"And when I called back it turned out that it was only a* **minor detail** *that had* **to be resolved** *in order to make the customer happy again."*

However, Wolf T. knows that no customer complaint should **be taken lightly**, *"You always have to react quickly. What's most important is to convey to the customer: I do what I can. Even if you can't* **drop everything***, you should make it clear to the customer that only he* **matters** *right now."*

## *Two customer groups*

Walter G., a sales representative for a commercial enterprise from Berlin, divides his customers into two groups: *the desperate ones* and the ones who *crave attention*. *"The latter ones use the opportunity to be the centre of attention. It's not so much about the **matter** itself. In contrast, the customers from the first group are really helpless and hope that someone **rescues them from** their plight."*

Conclusion: Professionally handled complaints present an excellent opportunity for expanding business with the customer. In Walter G.'s words, *"The happy ending of a complaint often means a new order."*

---

## Palabras para recordar

**complaint:** criticism, grievance, statement of dissatisfaction

---

**to respond:** to react, to take action

---

**upset:** annoyed, angry, irritated, exasperated, aggravated

---

**minor detail:** small, inconsequential, unimportant, or insignificant aspect

---

**to be resolved:** to be sorted out, settled, or worked out

---

**be taken lightly:** be treated carelessly, nonchalantly, or casually

---

**to drop everything:** to leave or abandon your work

---

**to matter:** to be of importance, to count, to be significant

---

**the desperate ones:** the frantic, anxious, distressed, or fraught ones

---

**to crave attention:** to long for, yearn for, or hunger after being noticed

---

**the latter ones:** the last-mentioned, the second-mentioned, the second of the two

---

**matter:** issue, question, problem, topic

---

**to rescue someone from:** to save someone from, to get

# *Only promise what you can keep*

*It is bad enough* when a customer *complains*. This is why you have to make sure that his problem, and *the aggravation that is coupled with it* will not increase.

*Play it safe* and only make promises to the customer which you can *faithfully* keep.

Following are some examples:

*Revert to* measures that are standard practise in your company or measures that you know *will be carried out* automatically. These can be:

- ✔ A colleague in the department, who is responsible for the product in question, calls the customer back within a (short) *predetermined* period of time.

- ✔ The customer receives the names and *extension* numbers of contact persons, in case he has *further inquiries.*

- ✔ A customer service representative arrives on location at the customer's during *an agreed-upon* maximum timeframe and is, of course, already precisely informed about the problem, so that the customer won't have to explain all the details once more.

- ✔ If the problem *concerns* the field sales force, they are to be informed immediately on their mobile phone. In case they are not available, leave the necessary information on their voice mail and ask for an immediate call-back. In addition, inform the customer about this and give him the sales representative's mobile phone number.

- ✔ You *assure* the customer that you will inform him within a certain timeframe about the *instant* measures that will be taken. If it *becomes apparent* that this may take a while, call the customer right away and let him know *the actual state of affairs*.

You can *extend* and complete this list just as you like. It is important, however, that this list *contains* only such *provisions that need to be carried out without fail*.

## *Display appropriate reactions*

Complaints are usually linked with *considerable annoyance* for the customers. The following sample sentences *are well-suited for* an initial reaction on the phone:

✔ *"I sympathise with you being annoyed* /I can very well understand you being annoyed."

✔ "I can understand that you *are angry about* this."

✔ "I understand very well why you are angry."

✔ "It is very understandable that you are exasperated about this."

✔ "Your disappointment about… is completely understandable."

✔ "We are very sorry/we very much regret that you're *experiencing such a hassle* because of…"

Examples of a written answer to a complaint:

✔ "You were complaining about… We are deeply sorry/we regret deeply that it has come to this."

✔ "You were complaining about… For any *inconvenience* that was caused to you as a result, *we sincerely apologise*."

✔ "We received your complaint about… *with great dismay*. We sincerely apologise for the trouble and inconvenience that this may have caused you."

|  | *Customer* | *Customer Service* Associate |
|---|---|---|
| Phrase 1 | "The **shipment** hasn't arrived yet! How much longer do we need to wait?" | (Listen **intently**, let the customer finish what he is saying, take notes.) |
| Phrase 2 |  | "I am deeply sorry, that is really **awfully troublesome**." (Develop your own **variation**.) |
| Phrase 3 | (Customer **quotes** a specific time.) | "When was the shipment supposed to arrive?" |
|  | (Customer speaks out on this.) | "Where you informed that there would be a **delay**?" |
| Phrase 4 |  | "So, the shipment was supposed to be there by... and has not yet arrived." |
| Phrase 5 |  | "Thank you very much for informing us about this. I will **arrange with... to** deliver immediately." (Inform the customer about the **unfolding** events.) |
| Phrase 6 |  | (Call the customers **to verify** that the shipment has arrived.) |

## Palabras para recordar

**to promise:** to guarantee, to assure, to pledge, to give one's word to

**it is bad enough:** it is unfortunate, unfavourable, or distressing to begin with

**to complain:** to protest, to find fault, to object, to carp, to make a fuss

**the aggravation that is coupled with it:** the annoyance, irritation, or stress that is connected with it

**to play it safe:** to take no chances, to stay out of danger, to take no risk

*(continúa)*

## *Continuación*

**faithfully:** loyally, truly, realistically

**to revert to something:** to fall back on, resort to, or make use of something

**will be carried out:** will be done, completed, accomplished, implemented, or executed

**predetermined:** fixed, set, prearranged, preagreed, predecided

**extension:** call-through, direct dial, direct access

**further inquiries:** additional, more, extra, new, or other questions

**an agreed-upon:** a decided, a settled, an arranged, an established, an approved

**to concern:** to affect, to relate to, to involve, to be about, to have to do with, to pertain to

**to assure:** to promise to, to declare to, to affirm to, to give one's word to

**instant:** immediate, on-the-spot, direct, prompt, instantaneous

**to become apparent:** to become clear, evident, obvious, plain, discernible, or noticeable

**the actual state of affairs:** how matters stand, what the current situation is

**to extend:** to expand, to lengthen, to increase in length, to continue

**to contain:** to hold, to include, to comprise, to involve, to incorporate

**provisions:** precautionary steps, measures, proceedings, or procedures

**that need to be carried out without fail:** that must be executed for certain, with certainty, or definitely

**appropriate:** proper, apt, suitable, correct

*(continúa)*

## *Continuación*

**considerable:** a great deal of, much, a lot of, a fair amount of

**annoyance:** irritation, frustration, exasperation, anger

**to be well-suited for:** to be good, right, or well qualified for

**I sympathise with you being annoyed:** I feel badly for you being angered, frustrated, or exasperated

**to be angry about something:** to be annoyed, irritated, gnashing one's teeth, or furious about something

**to experience such a hassle:** to go through, suffer, or encounter such difficulties

**inconvenience:** disruption, disturbance, trouble, worry, vexation

**we sincerely apologise:** we genuinely ask for forgiveness, we express our heartfelt regret

**with great dismay:** with utter consternation, with deep regret, with great concern

**associate:** colleague, fellow worker, co-worker, employee, member of staff

**shipment:** delivery, consignment

**intently:** closely, carefully, attentively, keenly

**awfully troublesome:** terribly upsetting, bothersome, annoying, irritating, or distressing

**variation:** version, alternative, variant, adaptation

**to quote:** to refer to, to cite, to give, to mention, to name

**delay:** late arrival, hold-up, wait, hindrance, obstruction

**to arrange with someone to do something:** to make preparations or plans for someone to do something

**unfolding:** developing, progressing, evolving

**to verify:** to make sure, to ensure, to confirm

# Opinion polls enhance customer satisfaction

If regular customer opinion polls become an integral part of your customer contact management, many problems *can be recognised* and solved before they start to show negative effects.

Basically, you may use *either* of the *main* versions of customer opinion polls:

✔ The all around opinion polls

This type of poll *covers* all relevant areas of business developments and customer relationships. It should *be conducted* in regular intervals in order to be able to recognise changes and any new developments early on.

This kind of poll serves *to determine* customer satisfaction in general – it does not refer to special *proceedings* such as handling complaints or service/guarantee orders. This type of poll should be conducted about once a year.

✔ The proceeding-oriented polls

It refers to a certain event and is carried out, for example, after a *repeat*, service, or guarantee *order*. It is important to perform the poll while the *occurrence* is still fresh in the customer's mind.

## Showing consideration *for the* customer

You should pay attention to the following points *to ensure* that customer polls *are not perceived as nuisance* but as a *courtesy*:

✔ ***Choose*** the right time for the poll. Do not conduct ***elaborate*** surveys before and immediately after important ***trade fairs*** which your customers are attending.

✔ Always tell your customers ahead of time about the poll. If you are conducting a written survey, call your customers beforehand and ask for their ***permission*** to question them. Doing so increases acceptance and results in a higher ***return rate***. If you plan to question customers about after-purchase services, prepare them during the purchasing process to let them know there will be a poll coming up. If polls are done verbally, proceed the other way around and send a letter to your customers, ***announcing*** the upcoming poll. In this message, you can point out how the customer will benefit if he chooses to participate.

✔ If you're interviewing customers over the telephone, make sure to ask if this is an ***opportune*** time to be questioned. If the customer seems stressed and ***restless***, ask if you should call back later.

✔ Limit your questions to the essentials. Even if you're conducting a major annual analysis, ***keep your questions in check***. The often recommended upper limit of three pages of A4-sized paper signals to the receiver that ***he has his work cut out for him***. It's better to limit the questions to one printed page.

✔ Make answering easy for the customer. ***Contrary to*** sales talks, closed questions are an advantage in polls because they are easier to answer. For example: The questions *"Would you recommend us?"* or *"Have you ever recommended us?"* can only be answered with *"yes"* or *"no."* However, if you ask *"What would be a reason for you to recommend us?"* it takes a while for the customer to think about it. There is another advantage to asking closed questions: Spontaneous replies ***tend to be more apt***. Therefore, test your ***questionnaire*** beforehand ***from that angle***. The quicker the test persons are able to answer it, the better.

## *To each his own way of questioning*

If you're conducting a customer-satisfaction analysis, it may be useful to ask individual customer groups in different ways.

Here are some examples:

- ✔ Ask *high-maintenance* customers, who need special solutions, *first and foremost* about their wishes and suggestions. Within this customer group, it may be beneficial to ask two or three open questions – provided they are asked in person and not on a questionnaire. It would be a good idea to offer discussion groups or conduct seminars for such "lead users."

- ✔ Customers, who require standard solutions and *place emphasis on smooth handling*, should be questioned on those subjects.

- ✔ Among customers, who willingly and frequently provide feedback, questionnaires may be unnecessary if you can find out more about them and their degree of satisfaction in personal contact. In this case, it may be best to take notes on their comments made over the phone or during a visit and transfer them into the database or use them for measures of improvement.

- ✔ You should interview reserved customers, who don't provide feedback and do not answer questionnaires, over the phone. If they react negatively to general "surveys," it is recommended to take advantage of concrete *occasions*, such as specialised services, to get them to talk freely in a personal conversation.

---

### Palabras para recordar

**opinion poll:** survey, review, sample, market research

**to enhance:** to improve, to increase, to add to, to augment, to boost

**can be recognised:** can be identified, made out, or spotted

*(continúa)*

### *Continuación*

**either:** both, each

**main:** major, chief, principal, most important

**to cover:** to include, to deal with, to contain, to comprise, to involve

**to be conducted:** to be carried out, performed, or done

**to determine:** to find out about, to clarify, to learn about

**proceedings:** measures, procedures, courses of action

**repeat order:** additional, extra, or recurring sale

**occurrence:** event, incident, circumstance, happening, proceeding

**to show consideration for someone:** to display thoughtfulness or respect for someone

**to ensure:** to make sure, to make certain, to warrant

**to not be perceived as:** to not be understood, identified, or regarded as

**nuisance:** irritation, annoyance, bother, inconvenience, pestering, harassment

**courtesy:** special treatment, thoughtfulness, attentiveness

**to choose:** to select, to pick, to decide on, to settle on, to designate

**elaborate:** complex, involved, extensive

**trade fair:** exhibition, exposition, show

**permission:** consent, authorisation, go-ahead, okay, agreement, say-so

**return rate:** feedback proportion, percentage, or ratio

**to announce:** to make known, to report, to disclose, to reveal

**opportune:** appropriate, favourable, apt, suitable, fitting

**restless:** uneasy, on edge, ill at ease, agitated

*(continúa)*

## *Continuación*

**to keep something in check:** to keep something within bounds, to not go overboard with something

**to have one's work cut out for oneself:** to have a big task or undertaking ahead of oneself

**contrary to:** in opposition to, at variance with, counter to, not in accord with

**to tend to be more apt:** to have a propensity to be true, correct, on target, or exactly right

**questionnaire:** survey, opinion

**from that angle:** from that perspective, viewpoint, standpoint, or point of view

**high-maintenance:** demanding, challenging, taxing

**first and foremost:** above all, first of all, in the first place

**to place emphasis on:** to put importance, attention, weight, or accent on

**smooth handling:** efficient or well-organised processing

**occasion:** event, occurrence, circumstance

# *Successful together for the long haul*

Long-term customer relationships may *be at risk* if you don't *perceive gradual changes*. Salespeople don't always *tap* the full potential of their existing customer relationships. They believe that they *have already opened up all possibilities* and they forget that long-term business relationships *in particular* and the *mode of collaboration* undergo change.

Following, management consultant Maria Kopelent from Regensburg explains: *"Business relationships are **sensitive** and*

*fragile entities*. *Often the **notion** of a harmonious relationship with the customer **prevails** because you've know each other so well for such a long time. However, your own company's re-organisation or internationalisation or that of your customers creates changes in different areas,"* says Kopelent. ***Aside from*** a continuous exchange of information with the customer, she recommends dialogue workshops with a neutral moderator. *"In a neutrally moderated process, people talk more openly and concretely about basic and trend-setting topics **beyond** the day-to-day business."* These are mainly:

✔ ***shared*** opportunities and developments,

✔ a shared understanding of the market and of the entire ***chain of processes***,

✔ sharing a common level and ***associating as peers***.

*"The expectations and **assumptions** as well as the ideas and wishes **voiced** on both sides create transparency about the **current** situation, the relationship's development and the **desire** for change on both sides,"* explains Maria Kopenent.

---

## Palabras para recordar

**for the long haul:** long-term, for a long time

**to be at risk:** to be in danger, in peril, or in jeopardy

**to perceive:** to recognise, to identify, to distinguish, to detect

**gradual changes:** slow but sure, step-by-step, or degree-by-degree transformations

**to tap:** to draw on, to use, to make use of, to utilise, to put to use, to exhaust, to exploit

**to have opened up all possibilities:** to have taken advantage of or utilised all options

*(continúa)*

### *Continuación*

**in particular:** especially, particularly, specifically

**mode of collaboration:** way, style, manner, or method of working together

**sensitive:** delicate, easily damaged, vulnerable

**fragile:** easily broken, insubstantial, breakable, fine

**entity:** thing, creation

**notion:** idea, view, conception, perception, thought, belief, impression

**to prevail:** to be in existence, prevalent, or current

**aside from:** in addition to, on top of, besides

**beyond:** outside the reach or limitations of, surpassing

**shared:** joint, multiparty, combined, common, collective, concerted

**chain of processes:** sequence of procedures, series of developments

**to associate as peers:** to mix, keep company, or deal with each other as equals

**assumption:** supposition, premise, belief, conjecture

**to voice:** to put in words, to express, to give utterance to, to articulate, to communicate

**current:** present, existing, ongoing, recent

**desire:** wish, inclination, eagerness, want, preference

# Vocabulario: inglés-español

• • • • • • • • • • • • • • • • • • • •

## A

**abandoned:** Abandonado

**accordingly:** Correspondientemente, de manera apropiada

**across borders:** En el extranjero

**adaptation:** Adaptación

**added value:** Valor añadido

**advancement:** Evolución

**affluent:** Ricas

**aggravating:** Irritante

**aids:** Ayudas

**all-terrain:** Todoterreno

**along the lines:** Del estilo

**amply:** Ampliamente

**apologetic:** Pedir disculpas

**appealing:** Interesante

**appears to be muddled:** Parece ser confuso

**are being alienated:** Enojarse

**are referred to:** Es remitido a

**are supposed to connect:** Se supone que conectan

**as a matter of principle:** Como principio

**assessment of collaboration:** Evaluación de colaboración

**associate:** Ayudante, compañero

**at any given time:** En todo momento

**auxiliary:** Auxiliar, complementario

**award of contract:** Concesión del contrato

## B

**be neglected:** Ser ignorado

**be taken lightly:** Tomarse a la ligera

**behaviour pattern:** Patrón de conducta

**binding guidelines:** Pautas de obligado cumplimiento

**bird can never fly wih one wing:** Ningún pájaro puede volar con una sola ala

**blocked off:** Cerradas

**broken down into:** Desglosados en

**buffer times:** Tiempos de interrupción

**business segments:** Segmentos empresariales

**buying syndicate:** Grupo de compras

## C

**can be marked off:** Poder dar por finalizado

**cartridge:** Cartucho

**chain of processes:** Cadena de procesos

**change for the worse:** Empeoramiento

**chart:** Gráfico

**checkout:** Caja

**commission statement:** Informes de comisiones

**common practice:** Práctica habitual

**complementary:** Complementarios

**complies with:** Cumple con

**comprehensibility:** Comprensión

**concealed:** Oculto

**concerted effort:** Esfuerzo combinado

**conjoint measurement:** Medida conjunta

**consent:** Consentimiento

**considerable:** Importante

**consistency:** Constancia

**containment:** Contención

**conviction:** Creencias

**copy-cat:** Imitación

**could be taken into consideration:** Podrían ser tomados en consideración

**cover letter:** Carátula

**credibility:** Credibilidad

**crowd:** Grupo

**cue:** Clave

## D

**deadline:** Plazo

**dealer:** Concesionario

**decisive for success:** Decisivas para tener éxito

**deep conviction:** Convicción profunda

**deep-frying:** Freír

**dependent on:** Dependiendo de

**depreciation:** Amortización

**desperate ones:** Los desesperados

**desperately needed:** Urgentemente necesaria

**diligence:** Diligencia

**dire times:** Tiempos difíciles

**disarming smile:** Sonrisa cautivadora

**distinct:** Inequívoca

**distribution channels:** Canales de distribución

**drugstore chain:** Cadena de farmacias

**durability:** Duración

## E

**embedding:** Incorporación

**enduring:** Duradero

**entity:** Asunto

**entrepreneur:** Empresario

**epitome of:** La personificación de

**exclusively:** Exclusivamente

**exemplary:** Ejemplar

**exhibition:** Exposición

**expedient:** Conveniente

**expenses for tied up capital:** Gastos por capital inmovilizado

## F

**fallacy:** Falacia

**fallback plan:** Plan de emergencia

**far too expensive:** Excesivamente costoso

**fear of failing:** Miedo al fracaso

**Federal Cross of Merit:** Cruz al Mérito Federal

**fiscal:** Fiscal

**focal point:** Centro de atención

**for the long haul:** A largo plazo

**for the purpose of:** Al objeto de

**fortification of trust:** Fortificación de la confianza

**fragile:** Frágil

**franchisee:** Beneficiario de una franquicia

**frictionless:** Sin tiranteces

**from floor to ceiling:** Desde el suelo hasta el techo

**from the vicinity of:** De los alrededores de

**full extent:** Todo el alcance

**full to the brim:** Hasta arriba

## G

**generously spending:** Gasto generoso

**grab it straightaway:** Aprovecharlo inmediatamente

**gradual changes:** Cambios graduales

**grant:** Subvención

**grave:** Cruciales

**gut-feeling:** Instinto

## H

**head of accounting:** Jefe de contabilidad

**heartfelt notion:** El sincero concepto

**high repute:** Buena reputación

**human resources:** Recursos humanos

## I

**if you want to last in business:** Si desea seguir en el negocio

**immediacy:** Cercanía

**imperatively:** Imperativamente

**in accord with:** Estar de acuerdo con

**in concurrence with:** De acuerdo con

**in making this added value visible:** Hacer notorio el valor añadido

**in the lead-up:** Con anterioridad

**incident:** Incidente

**inclusion:** Inclusión

**independently from:** Independientemente de

**indolence:** Indolencia

**intently imagined:** Imaginado vívidamente

**inter-coordinated:** Inter-coordinados

**introduction:** Introducción

**invoiced:** Facturados

**is accomplished:** Conseguirse

**is supposed to:** Ser supuestamente para

**is the gist of what:** Es la esencia

**is to be executed:** Debe llevarse a cabo

**it could be assumed:** Se podría dar por supuesto

**it has not failed us yet:** Todavía no nos ha fallado

**it was a done deal:** Todo estaba cerrado

## J

**jealousy:** Envidia

**jeopardised:** En peligro

## L

**lateness:** Impuntualidad

**latter ones:** Estos últimos

**leaflet:** Folletos

**limited liability company:** Sociedad de responsabilidad limitada

**line of goods:** Línea de producto

**long-term retention:** Retención a largo plazo

## M

**maintenance:** Mantenimiento

**map:** Mapa

**meaningless:** Carentes de sentido

**membership:** Ser miembro

**merger:** Fusiones

**misconceived:** Mal concebida

**mode of collaboration:** Estilo de colaboración

**more confident:** Con mayor confianza

**more customer-friendly approach:** Un enfoque más orientado hacia el cliente

**more distinct:** Más singular

**more inclined:** Más predispuestos

**more than what one can put up with:** Más de los que se pueden tolerar

**most malicious:** La más maliciosa

**most notable:** Las más notables

## N

**necessities:** Necesidades

**need to be prevailed over:** Deberse superar

**newness:** Novedad

**noticeably restricted:** Acusadamente limitado

**notion:** Idea

**notorious:** Famoso

## O

**objective targets:** Metas objetivas

**of endeavouring towards:** De esforzarse por

**office supply costs:** Costes de suministros de oficina

**old hand:** Perro viejo

**on an average of:** Una media de

**on the spot:** En el lugar

**on the spur of the moment:** Al momento

**overview at the push of a button:** Panorámica general a un clic del *mouse*

## P

**partial:** Parcial

**phrase-mongering:** Jerigonza

**pillar:** Pilar

**pivotal point:** Punto fundamental

**planned/actual comparison:** Comparación entre la previsión y la realidad

**plight:** Apuro

**point of intersection:** Punto de intersección

**polite:** Educadas

**postal code:** Código postal

**precipitate:** Precipitadas

**predicament:** Problemas

**pricing as a competitive factor competitive:** Precio como factor de competitividad competitivo

**principal agent:** Representante principal

**printed impression:** Imagen impresa

**procurement:** Abastecimiento

**pronounced:** Acusado

**proximity:** Proximidad

**punctuality:** Puntualidad

**purest of intentions:** Las intenciones más puras

**pursued:** Buscados

**pushy:** Agresivo

## R

**rallying cry:** Lema

**realisable:** Factible

**recipient:** Receptor

**reciprocal:** Recíproca

**recovery:** Recuperación

**registered association largely:** Asociación registrada fundamentalmente

**reluctantly:** A regañadientes

**renowned:** Renombrados

**reusable:** Reutilizable

**reward:** Recompensa

**ruinous competitive battles:** Luchas competitivas desastrosas

**ruthlessly:** Sin piedad

## S

**sales-boosting:** Potenciadora de las ventas

**same parts management:** Gestión de piezas iguales

**sanitary facilities:** Instalaciones sanitarias

**seasonably:** Estacionalmente

**seasoned pro:** Profesional experimentado

**selective use:** Uso selectivo

**similar issues:** Cuestiones parecidas

**simple virtues:** Cualidades sencillas

**simplified:** Simplificada

**sole:** Único

**something encouraging:** Algo estimulante

**something is abandoned:** Abandonar algo

**sought-after:** Cortejado

**spare parts kit:** Conjunto de piezas de repuesto

**special request:** Petición especial

**steep:** Alto

**still need to be developed:** Aún es necesario seguir insistiendo

**stinginess is cool:** La tacañería es genial

**storage:** Almacenamiento

**subconscious:** Subconsciente

**subconsciously:** Subconscientemente

**subliminal:** Subliminal

**sub-segment:** Subsegmento

**subsidiary:** Filial

**suggestion for improvement:** Sugerencias de mejora

**superb:** Magnífica

**superfluous:** Superfluas

**survival:** Supervivencia

## T

**tardy:** Impuntual

**target agreement:** Acuerdo de objetivos

**technical term:** Término técnico

**terms & conditions:** Términos y condiciones

**than suspected:** De lo que se imaginan

**that he actually does take centre stage:** De que él es realmente el centro de atención

**that may all be fine and dandy:** Eso parece perfecto

**they knew from experience:** Saber por experiencia

**to abstain from:** Abstenerse de

**to accord to:** Ofrecer

**to adress:** Dirigirse a

**to advise against something:** Desaconsejar algo

**to afford:** Ofrecer

**to allure:** Atraer

**to amend:** Modificar

**to annotate:** Añadir notas a

**to appoint:** Designar

**to appreciate someone:** Valorar a alguien

**to appreciate something greatly:** Apreciar algo enormemente

**to arise:** Surgir

**to associate as peers:** Asociarse en pie de igualdad

**to attempt:** Intentar

**to attune to:** Adaptarse a

**to be a native of:** Ser natural de

**to be a no-no for someone:** Ser inaceptable para alguien

**to be advantageous:** Ser útil

**to be agreeable towards:** Parecerle bien

**to be at risk:** Peligrar

**to be attuned to:** Estar en sintonía

**to be bothersome:** Ser engorrosos

**to be bound to fail:** Seguramente fracasar

**to be cajoled into something:** Dejarse engatusar

**to be completely unfounded:** Carecer totalmente de fundamento

**to be custom tailored to:** Estar adaptada a las necesidades de

**to be deprived of:** Carecer de

**to be determined:** Tomar una determinación

**to be disclosed to one:** Serle revelado a uno

**to be eager:** Estar ansioso

**to be even more essential:** Ser aún más importante

**to be exemplified by:** Quedar de manifiesto por

**to be faced with a challenge:** Enfrentarse a un reto

**to be genuinely interested:** Estar realmente interesado

**to be greatly tempted:** Sentir la tentación

**to be in charge of something:** Estar a cargo de algo

**to be in need of explanation:** Necesitar explicación

**to be in touch with something:** Estar en contacto con algo

**to be less of a concern:** Ser de menor preocupación

**to be maintained:** Mantenerse

**to be meliorated:** Ser perfeccionadas

**to be more sensible:** Ser más sensato

**to be obligated:** Estar obligados a

**to be on the look out for:** Estar ojo avizor

**to be overly zealous:** Mostrar exceso de celo

**to be perceived objectively:** Ser percibido de forma objetiva

**to be promising:** Ser prometedores

**to be prone to breaking down:** Tener predisposición a estropearse

**to be pure luck:** Ser pura suerte

**to be quite varied:** Ser bastante diversos

**to be readily available:** Ser fácilmente accesible

**to be responsible for something:** Ser responsable de algo

**to be retired:** Estar jubilado

**to be so dumbfounded:** Quedarse tan asombrado

**to be the way to go:** Ser el camino que hay que seguir

**to be very determined:** Estar claramente decidido

**to be virtually ubiquitous:** Ser casi omnipresente

**to be wrested:** Ser arrebatado

**to bear fruit:** Dar fruto

**to beat one to the punch:** Adelantársele a alguien

**to become annoyed:** Enfadarse

**to become apparent:** Hacerse evidente

**to become aware of something:** Conocer

**to bemoan:** Lamentarse de

**to bid farewell to something:** Decirle adiós a algo

**to bless:** Bendecir

**to blossom:** Transformarse en

**to calm someone down nit-picker:** Calmar a alguien quisquilloso, puntilloso

**to campaign:** Luchar por

**to cater precisely to:** Atender precisamente a

**to channel:** Canalizar

**to cheer up:** Animarse

**to climb the social ladder:** Subir en la escala social

**to coax someone out of one's shell:** Hacer salir a alguien de su cascarón

**to come across as pushy:** Parecer agresivo

**to come away empty-handed:** Terminar con las manos vacías

**to come to an interesting conclusion:** Llegar a una conclusión interesante

**to compare notes:** Intercambiar opiniones

**to complete:** Completar

**to concern oneself with something:** Preocuparse por algo

**to consist solely of:** Incluir únicamente

**to consolidate:** Consolidar

**to constrain:** Constreñir

**to corner someone:** Acorralar a alguien

**to correlate:** Guardar correlación

**to crave attention:** Reclamar atención

**to cross the 50s threshold:** Atravesar el umbral de los 50 años

**to crumble:** Desintegrar

**to cut down:** Reducir

**to cut off:** Interrumpir

**to decrease:** Disminuir

**to devalue:** Devaluar

**to dig deep into one's pockets:** Rascarse el bolsillo

**to display extra caution:** Tener una precaución especial

**to dispose of something:** Deshacerse de algo

**to disregard:** Pasar por alto

**to distinguish oneself from:** Diferenciarse de

**to distinguish oneself from someone:** Diferenciarse de alguien

**to do something to prompt someone:** Inducir a alguien a hacer algo

**to draw one's conclusions:** Extraer conclusiones

**to drop everything:** Dejarlo todo

**to elucidate:** Esclarecer, aclarar

**to embark on:** Emprender

**to embrace:** Aceptar

**to enable:** Posibilitar, permitir

**to enter into:** Introducir en

**to enter unknown territory:** Entrar en un terreno desconocido

**to entertain considerable doubt:** Albergar muchas dudas

**to equip:** Equipar

**to expect a great deal:** Ser muy exigente

**to experience defeat:** Sufrir una derrota

**to fear:** Temer

**to feed someone's hopes:** Alimentar las esperanzas de alguien

**to feel hassled:** Sentirse molesto

**to feel more obligated:** Sentirse más obligado

**to feel uneasy:** Sentirse incómodo

**to figure something out:** Entender algo

**to firmly root:** Arraigar con firmeza

**to fulfil their mission:** Llevar a cabo su misión

**to gain traction on:** Conseguir acceso a

**to get the bid:** Conseguir la oferta

**to get to the bottom of the matter:** Llegar al fondo de la cuestión

**to give someone similarly high marks:** Otorgar a alguien unas calificaciones igualmente elevadas

**to go into something:** Ocuparse de algo

**to go without saying:** Ser completamente normal

**to greatly amplify:** Aumentar enormemente

**to hail from:** Ser de

**to hang on:** Aguantar sin cejar

**to hardly differ:** Diferir apenas

**to haul in:** Generar

**to have a knack for something:** Tener un don para algo

**to have at one's disposal:** Tener a disposición de uno

**to have come up with:** Idear

**to have good taste:** Tener buen gusto

**to have opened up all possibilities:** Haber aprovechado todas las posibilidades

**to have to grapple with something:** Tener que esforzarse por resolver algo

**to have to struggle through:** Tener que esforzarse mucho

**to heat up:** Calentar

**to help oneself to:** Quedarse con

**to hijack:** Apropiarse de

**to hurt no one:** No perjudicar a nadie

**to illustrate:** Ilustrar

**to inspect:** Inspeccionar

**to intently concern oneself with:** Estar muy interesado en

**to internalize something:** Interiorizar algo

**to inundate:** Inundar

**to issue:** Distribuir

**to jam:** Bloquear

**to keep cropping up:** Suceder

**to label as:** Calificar como

**to lack the motivation:** Falta de motivación

**to let oneself in for something:** Dejarse atrapar

**to level the price down:** Reducir el precio

**to link:** Conectar

**to make a face:** Hacer muecas

**to make someone suspicious:** Hacerle a alguien desconfiar

**to make up one's mind to do something:** Tomar la decisión de hacer algo

**to no longer be content:** Ya no basta

**to nod:** Asentir con la cabeza

**to not be a constant:** No ser una constante

**to not be able to pull the wool oversomeone's eyes:** No poder engañar a alguien

**to not be adding value:** Que no añaden valor

**to not be afraid of something:** No tener miedo de

**to not be aware of something:** No ser consciente de algo

**to not be completely done in:** No estar completamente agotado

**to not be content:** No estar satisfecho

**to not be rushed for time:** No andar apresurado

**to not be willing:** No estar dispuestos a

**to not comply with:** No satisfacer

**to not fall by the wayside:** No perderse por el camino

**to not lapse into:** No adquirir

**to not let oneself be put off:** No dejarse disuadir

**to not need to bother:** No ser necesario molestarse

**to not stand out:** No destacar

**to omit:** Omitir

**to open up new vistas:** Abrir nuevas miras

**to open up:** Abrir

**to outweigh:** Compensar

**to overcome:** Superar

**to overextend oneself:** Extralimitarse

**to pass the time:** Pasar el tiempo

**to pave the way for something:** Preparar el camino

**to pay attention to someone:** Prestar atención a alguien

**to pay heed to:** Prestar atención

**to peruse something:** Leer algo detenidamente

**to preclude:** Impedir

**to preferentially assign:** Asignar preferentemente

**to procrastinate in doing something:** Posponer indefinidamente la realización de algo

**to procrastinate:** Posponer

**to propose:** Proponer

**to prove to be:** Resultar

**to push through:** Lograr la aceptación

**to put good ideas into action:** Poner en práctica las buenas ideas

**to put on the back burner:** Dejar en suspenso por el momento

**to put someone in their place:** Poner a alguien en su sitio

**to put someone off:** Desanimar

**to quadruple:** Cuadruplicarse

**to recall from memory:** Traer a la memoria

**to recapture:** Recuperar

**to recruit:** Contratar

**to refrain from:** Evitar

**to remain unresponsive to something:** Permanecer indiferente a algo

**to render:** Prestar

**to rephrase:** Reformular

**to replace:** Reemplazar

**to reprimand:** Castigarse

**to rescue someone from:** Rescatar a alguien de

**to ring hollow:** Sonar falso

**to run into a lot of money:** Consumir mucho dinero

**to safely assume something:** Suponer con seguridad algo

**to seek advice from:** Buscar consejo en

**to seem suspicious:** Parecer sospechosa

**to shrink:** Reducirse

**to sink deep into one's memory:** Memorizar bien a fondo

**to stay true to someone:** Mantenerse fiel a alguien

**to stem from something:** Ser producto de

**to stem from:** Provenir de

**to stick to one's guns:** Mantenerse firme

**to stick to one's set objectives:** Atenerse a los objetivos que uno se ha marcado

**to strike the right note:** Dar en el clavo

**to substantiate:** Demostrar

**to substituted by:** Sustituir por

**to substitute for:** Sustituir por

**to surround oneself with:** Dejar que algo se contagie

**to survive:** Sobrevivir

**to take a new run at it:** Intentarlo de nuevo

**to take one's time:** Tomarse su tiempo

**to tap:** Aprovechar

**to trace:** Seguir

**to tune out:** Dejar de prestar atención

**to unburden:** Descargar

**to undercut:** Bajar

**to undergo change:** Experimentar cambios

**to utter:** Pronunciar

**to valorise:** Potenciar

**to ward off:** Protegerse contra

**to weave:** Tejer

**tremendous:** Enorme

**truth dawned on him:** Se da cuenta de la realidad

# U

**unique:** Única

**unknown entity:** Organismo desconocido

**unmistakable:** Inconfundible

**used-up:** Usado

**utmost:** Mayor

## V

**variant:** Alternativa

**various sources:** Diversas fuentes

**victim:** Una víctima

## W

**was commissioned:** Se le encargó

**wastage:** Pérdida

**were to be taken into account:** Fueron tomados en cuenta

**what do I get out of it:** En qué me beneficia

**whereabouts:** Paradero

**wholesale:** Al por mayor

**words of salutation:** Palabras de saludo

# Glosario

• • • • • • • • • • • • • • • • • • • • • • • •

**abandoned:** dropped, done without, given up, put aside, relinquished → 42, 44, 58-59, 129, 134

**accordingly:** appropriately, correspondingly, properly, suitably → 6, 8, 80, 83, 129

**across borders:** in foreign, far-off, or distant countries, overseas → 65-66, 68, 129

**actual state of affairs:** how matters stand, what the current situation is → 117, 120

**added value:** additional or extra worth → 14-15, 74, 76, 129, 132

**advancement:** progress, improvement, development, furtherance → 105-106, 129

**affluent:** wealthy, well-to-do, well off, moneyed → 90, 92, 129

**aggravating:** frustrating, irritating, annoying, getting on one's nerves → 28, 30, 129

**aggravation that is coupled with it:** the annoyance, irritation, or stress that is connected with it → 117, 119

**aids:** means, tools, resources → 6, 62, 87-88, 129

**all-terrain:** cross-country → 95, 97, 129

**along the lines:** within the framework or bounds, in the context → 51-52, 129

**amply:** sufficiently, adequately, abundantly → 37, 39, 129

**an agreed-upon:** a decided, a settled, an arranged, an established, an approved → 117, 120

**apologetic:** remorseful, contrite, regretful → 7, 9, 129

**appealing:** likeable, pleasing, interesting, engaging → 96-98, 129

**appears to be muddled:** seems to be messed up, tangled, or in shambles → 104, 106, 129

**applicable:** relevant, appropriate, pertinent, valid → 90, 92

**are referred to:** are directed, forwarded, sent, or transferred to → 82, 84, 129

**are supposed to connect:** should link up with one another → 104, 106

**as a matter of principle:** basically, on principle → 84-85, 129

**assessment of collaboration:** evaluation of teamwork or partnership → 63-64, 129

**associate:** colleague, fellow worker, co-worker, employee, member of staff → 28, 35, 63, 119, 121, 128-129, 135

**at any given time:** at all times, all the time, each time, every time → 93-94, 129

**auxiliary:** additional, supplementary, extra, secondary, supporting, ancillary, added → 16, 75-76, 81, 83, 129

**award of contract:** contract award process, placing of orders → 19, 21, 129

**awfully troublesome:** terribly upsetting, bothersome, annoying, irritating, or distressing → 119, 121

**be neglected:** be ignored, looked over, disregarded, forgotten, or avoided → 33, 35, 129

**be taken lightly:** be treated carelessly, nonchalantly, or casually → 115-116, 129

**behaviour pattern:** way of acting, system of conduct, comportment, deportment, or bearing → 54, 129

**binding guidelines:** compulsory, obligatory, or requisite rules → 58-9, 129

**bird can never fly with one wing:** you cannot stand while having only one foot on the ground → 104, 106

**blocked off:** closed off, cordoned off, barricaded, fenced off → 96, 98, 130

**breach of agreements:** breaking, violating, or contravention of contracts → 109, 112

**broken down into:** separated, categorised, classified, or itemised into → 93-94, 130

**buffer times:** leeway, elbowroom, latitude. room to move, breathing space → 60-61, 130

**buying syndicate:** purchasing association or group → 44, 130

**can be marked off:** can be finished, completed, done, concluded, accomplished, or fulfilled → 61, 130

**can be recognised:** can be identified, made out, or spotted → 122, 124

**cancellation notice:** letter of annulment, termination, or cessation → 111-112

**cartridge:** cassette, container → 30, 130

**chain of processes:** sequence of procedures, series of developments → 127-128, 130

**change for the worse:** a deterioration, decline, or weakening → 56-57, 130

**checkout:** cash point, cash register → 46, 48, 130

**collector's value:** saver's or accumulator's worth → 14, 17

**commission statement:** percentage receipt, compensation record → 75, 130

**common practice:** customary, everyday, routine, or standard procedure → 86, 88, 130

**complementary:** accompanying, supplementary → 82, 84, 130

**complies with:** adheres to, conforms to, acquiesces with, assents to, meets the terms of → 32, 35, 130

**concealed:** hidden, out of sight, unnoticed, obscured → 36, 39, 130

**concerted effort:** combined, joint, or collaborative operation → 62, 64

**conjoint measurement:** united, connected, or combined analysis → 33, 35, 130

**connected with:** linked to, associated with, related to → 21, 109, 112, 119

**consciousness:** mind, thoughts, awareness, memory, cognizance → 103

**consent:** permission, go-ahead, authority, agreement, sanction → 9, 90, 92, 112, 125, 130

**considerably:** significantly, very much, a great deal, substantially → 27, 29, 75

**consistency:** constancy, steadiness, stability, dependability → 48-49, 51, 130

**containment:** control, restriction, regulation, limitation → 33, 35, 130

**contrary to:** in opposition to, at variance with, counter to, not in accord with → 123, 126

**copy-cat:** imitator, copier → 72, 130

**could be taken into consideration:** could be included, regarded, kept in mind, or incorporated → 91-92, 130

**courtesy:** special treatment, thoughtfulness, attentiveness → 122, 125

**cover letter:** first page of the written message → 87, 89, 130

**credibility:** trustworthiness, reliability, integrity, authority, standing → 103, 105-106, 130

**crowd:** group, set, circle, clique → 101, 103, 130

**cue:** hint, signal, sign, intimation, indication → 35, 130

**deadline:** time limit, cut-off-date, target → 24, 26, 130

**dealer:** trader, wholesaler → 75, 97, 130

**decisive:** deciding, determining, critical → 10

**decisive for success:** important, crucial, influential, or key for victory → 33, 35, 130

**deep-frying:** cooking → 69-70, 72, 130

**demeanour:** manner, conduct, behaviour → 10

**dependent on:** conditional on, contingent on, determined by, subject to → 91-92, 130

**depreciation:** decrease, lowering, or reduction in value → 37, 39, 130

**desperate ones:** the frantic, anxious, distressed, or fraught ones → 116, 130

**desperately needed:** very much, greatly or urgently required → 38-39, 130

**deteriorating:** worsening, declining, going downhill, weakening → 109, 112

**diligence:** assiduity, industriousness, heedfulness, laboriousness, conscientiousness → 48-49, 51, 130-131

**dire times:** bad, difficult, trying, tough, dismal, dreadful, or critical spell → 78-79, 131

**disarming smile:** charming, persuasive, or winning beam → 8, 10, 131

**discord:** friction, disagreement, difference of opinion, dissension, conflict → 110, 113

**distinct:** clear, unmistakeable, definite, recognisable, palpable, noticeable, plain → 20, 22, 47, 131, 133

**distribution channels:** sales means, media, vehicles, or routes → 40, 42-43, 131

**drugstore chain:** chemist's shop franchise or group → 61, 63, 131

**durability:** permanence, durableness, long-lastingness, soundness → 56-57, 131

**durable consumer goods:** long-lasting, hard-wearing, or strong end-user commodities → 14, 17

**enduring:** lasting, continuing, stable → 78-79, 131

**ensured:** made sure, made certain, guaranteed, warranted → 60, 109, 112

**entity:** thing, creation → 37, 39, 128, 131, 142

**entrepreneur:** businessman, business owner, enterpriser → 66, 68, 131

**epitome of:** the essence, quintessence, embodiment, or archetype of → 95, 97, 131

**error in invoicing:** mistake, inaccuracy, or miscalculation in billing → 112,

**exclusively:** solely, only → 28, 30, 45, 131

**exemplary:** excellent, commendable, very good, model, ideal → 61, 63, 131

**expenses for tied up capital:** cost of the employed capital, associated costs → 32, 35, 131

**faithfully:** loyally, truly, realistically → 117, 119-120

**fallacy:** misleading notion, erroneous belief, false conclusion, misconception, misjudgement → 37, 39, 131

**far too expensive:** much too, by a great amount too, or markedly too costly → 81, 83, 131

**fear of failing:** worry about not succeeding, falling short, or not making the grade → 51-52

**Federal Cross of Merit:** one of the highest honours the Federal Republic of Germany awards → 62, 64, 131

**first and foremost:** above all, first of all, in the first place → 124, 126

**fiscal:** business, financial, economic → 97-98, 102, 131

**focal point:** focus, emphasis, main focus, main area of concern → 45, 91-92, 106, 131

**for a surcharge:** for an additional price, for extra cost → 16, 18

**for the long haul:** long-term, for a long time → 126-127, 131

**for the purpose of:** as defined by, in the sense of → 41, 44, 131

**fortification of trust:** strengthening or reinforcement of confidence → 105, 107, 131

**fragile:** easily broken, insubstantial, breakable, fine → 126-128, 131

**franchisee:** one who is given a warrant, charter, or license → 67, 69, 131

**frictionless:** smooth, unobstructed, trouble-free → 104, 106, 131

**from floor to ceiling:** from the ground to the roof, from the botton up → 62-63, 131

**from that angle:** from that perspective, viewpoint, standpoint, or point of view → 123, 126

**from the vicinity of:** from the surrounding area, neighbourhood, locality, or district of → 66, 68, 131

**full extent:** the complete scale, degree, or magnitude → 24, 26, 131

**full to the brim:** filled up, full to capacity → 57, 59, 131

**further inquiries:** additional, more, extra, new, or other questions → 117, 120

**generously spending:** liberally splurging or consuming → 100, 102, 131

**grab it straightaway:** seize the opportunity immediately, at once, right away, or without delay → 20, 22, 131

**gradual changes:** slow but sure, step-by-step, or degree-by-degree transformations → 126-127, 131

**grant:** partial funding or allowance, stipend, subvention → 79, 131

**grave:** vital, crucial, critical, serious, significant → 66, 68, 131

**gut-feeling:** guess, hunch, instinct, intuition → 54-55, 131-132

**head of accounting:** chief, director, manager, or person in charge of bookkeeping → 93-94, 132

**heartfelt notion:** the sincere, genuine, profound, or deep belief → 105-106, 132

**high-maintenance:** demanding, challenging, taxing → 124, 126

**high repute:** good name, high standing or stature, good reputation → 61, 63, 132

**human resources:** personnel, staff, employees, workers, workforce → 37, 39, 132

**I sympathise with you being annoyed:** I feel badly for you being angered, frustrated, or exasperated → 118, 121

**if you want to last in business:** if you desire to continue, carry on, remain, or keep on in commerce → 93-94, 132

**immediacy:** nearness, closeness, propinquity → 103, 105, 132

**imperative:** very important, crucial, necessary, indispensable, vital → 9

**imperatively:** coercively, stringently, strictly, rigorously → 105-106, 132

**impolite:** rude, ill-mannered, bad-mannered, discourteous, ungracious → 109, 112

**in accord with:** in concurrence, agreement, or accordance with → 104, 106, 126, 132, 145

**in the lead-up:** prior, earlier, in advance → 81, 83, 132

**incident:** unpleasant occurrence or happening → 36-37, 39, 125, 132

**inclusion:** incorporation, integration → 42, 44, 132

**inconvenience:** disruption, disturbance, trouble, worry, vexation → 118, 121, 125

**independently from:** separately from, unrelated to, detached from → 100, 102, 132

**indolence:** inactivity, laziness, sluggishness, idleness → 69, 72, 132

**intently:** closely, carefully, attentively, keenly → 121

**inter-coordinated:** aligned, balanced → 78-79

**introduction:** launch, presentation, promotion → 46, 95, 97, 132

**invoiced:** billed, charged, debited → 40, 43, 132

**is accomplished:** is achieved, pulled off, realised, or brought about → 46, 48, 132

**is supposed to:** is meant, intended, or designed to → 46, 62, 64, 132

**is the gist of what:** is the general idea, essence, or quintessence of what → 63-64, 132

**is to be executed:** is to be carried out, accomplished, or achieved → 57, 59, 132

**it could be assumed:** it could be taken for granted, presupposed, presumed, or believed → 95, 97, 132

**it has not failed us yet:** it has not let us down or disappointed us so far → 27, 30, 132

**it is bad enough:** it is unfortunate, unfavourable, or distressing to begin with → 116-117, 119

**it was a done deal:** everything was accepted, settled, given a positive response, or agreed to → 70, 72, 132

**jealousy:** envy, resentment, covetousness, resentfulness → 36, 38-39, 132

**jeopardised:** threatened, imperilled, vulnerable → 103, 105, 132

**justification:** good reason, explanation, rationalisation → 16, 18

**lacking adherence to delivery dates:** failing to distribute merchandise on time or punctually → 109, 112

**latter ones:** the last-mentioned, the second-mentioned, the second of the two → 116, 132

**leaflet:** booklet, brochure, pamphlet, flier → 88, 132

**leeway:** room to manoeuvre, room to operate, elbowroom, freedom, flexibility → 10

**limited liability company:** corporation, private limited company → 40, 43, 132

**line of goods:** range or assortment of goods, product line, line of merchandise → 71-73, 132

**long-term retention:** lasting preservation, longstanding maintenance → 100, 102, 132

**low tendency to break down:** slight inclination or propensity to stop working → 14, 17

**maintenance:** servicing, overhaul, check → 12-13, 17, 82, 98, 102, 110, 132-133

**map:** chart, plan → 91-92, 133

**may be created by:** may be produced or generated by, may be a result of → 17-18

**meaningless:** valueless, empty, futile → 23, 25, 133

**measurable:** assessable, estimable, appraisable, fathomable → 109, 112

**membership:** participation, involvement → 96-98, 133

**merger:** amalgamation, fusion, joining, combination, union → 43, 133

**misconceived:** imagined, misinterpreted, misunderstood → 23, 25, 133

**mode of collaboration:** way, style, manner, or method of working together → 126, 128, 133

**more confident:** the more sure, positive, convinced, or secure → 93-94, 133

**more customer-friendly approach:** an extra client-responsive manner or style → 40, 43, 133

**more inclined:** the more willing, ready, predisposed, prone, or liable → 82, 84, 133

**more than what one can put up with:** more than what one can endure, bear, or tolerate → 85, 133

**most malicious:** the most harmful, hurtful, or destructive → 38-39, 133

**most notable:** the most noteworthy, important, or significant → 58-59, 133

**necessities:** needs, requirements, requisites, essentials → 38, 40, 133

**need to be prevailed over:** must be surmounted, overcome, or conquered → 46-48, 133

**newness:** inventiveness, freshness, innovation, originality, novelty → 47

**noticeably restricted:** distinctly or markedly limited → 100, 103

**notion:** idea, view, conception, perception, thought, belief, impression → 39, 105-106, 127-128, 132-133

**notorious:** legendary, famous, renowned → 24, 26, 133

**nuisance:** irritation, annoyance, bother, inconvenience, pestering, harassment → 122, 125

**objective targets:** aims, goals → 38, 40, 133

**occurrence:** event, incident, circumstance, happening, proceeding → 39, 122, 125-126

**of endeavouring towards:** of striving for, of trying one's hand at, of attempting, of making an effort for → 104, 106, 133

**office supply costs:** expenses for place of work resources → 28, 30, 133

**old hand:** veteran, expert, old-timer, master → 73, 133

**on an average of:** typically in the region of, more or less around → 73, 75-76, 133

**on the spot:** on the scene, locally, on location, on site → 89, 91, 133

**on the spur of the moment:** at first go, right away, straight away → 77, 80, 133

**overview at the push of a button:** overall view or general idea at a mouse click → 93-94, 133

**paragraph:** section, part, item → 88, 89

**partial:** fractional, limited, fragmentary → 50, 52, 79, 133

**particular:** specific, individual → 10

**permission:** consent, authorisation, go-ahead, agreement, okay, say-so → 92, 109, 112, 123, 125

**phrase-mongering:** hot air, waffling, flannelling, gobbledygook → 106, 133

**pivotal point:** central point, focal point → 104, 106, 133

**planned/actual comparison:** contrast of intended and confirmed data → 94-95, 133

**point of intersection:** meeting or crossing point, juncture, node → 105, 134

**polite:** diplomatic, polished, tactful, subtle, suave → 8, 113-114, 134

**postal code:** zip code, post code → 91-92, 134

**precipitate:** hurried, impulsive → 77, 80, 134

**predicament:** problem, challenge, trouble → 77, 80, 134

**preparatory work:** preliminary, introductory, or basic effort → 110, 113

**preservation of value:** maintenance, continuation, upholding, keeping of worth → 14, 17

**principal agent:** chief or general representative → 66, 68, 134

**printed impression:** print image, printed design → 28, 30, 134

**processed:** sorted out, handled, → 109, 112

**procurement:** purchasing, resource acquisition → 41, 44, 134

**pronounced:** apparent, distinct, evident → 46-47, 134

**provisions:** precautionary steps, measures, proceedings, or procedures → 76, 118, 120

**proximity:** nearness, adjacency, vicinity, propinquity, closeness → 89, 91, 134

**purest of intentions:** honourable, upright, or decent objectives → 105-106, 134

**pursued:** chased, worked at, aimed at, engaged in → 101, 103, 134

**rallying cry:** slogan, catchword, motto → 40, 43, 134

**rather than with:** instead with, more readily than with → 15, 18

**recipient:** receiver, addressee → 87, 89, 134

**reciprocal:** mutual, give-and-take, joint, shared, equal, corresponding → 66, 68, 134

**recovery:** growth, boom, boost, upturn → 77-78, 134

**refurbishing:** renovating, restoring, revamping, overhauling, making over → 14, 17

**regardless:** at any rate, in any case, anyhow, no matter what → 10

**registered association:** registered as recorded club, society, organisation, or group → 98, 134

**reluctantly:** unwillingly, half-heartedly, grudgingly, unenthusiastically → 6, 8, 134

**renowned:** famous, distinguished, well-known, prominent, established → 26, 62-63

**repeat order:** additional, extra, or recurring sale → 125

**resale value:** worth of something being sold again → 14, 17

**resolved:** answered, sorted out, cleared up → 30

**restless:** uneasy, on edge, ill at ease, agitated → 123, 125

**retention measures:** preservation or maintenance actions → 107, 110

**return rate:** feedback proportion, percentage, or ratio → 123, 125

**reusable:** returnable, multi-use → 71, 73, 134

**reward:** recompense, remuneration, bonus, prize → 17, 62, 64, 134

**ruthlessly:** mercilessly, unmercifully, pitilessly, remorselessly → 36, 38, 134

**sales-boosting:** sales-increasing, improving, amplifying, enlarging, expanding, or advancing → 67, 69, 134

**same parts management:** identical, equal, or matching components supervision → 32, 35, 134

**sanitary facilities:** bathroom fixtures and fittings → 73, 75, 134

**seasonably:** appropriate to the time of the year → 62-63, 134

**seasoned pro:** an experienced, a well versed, an established, or a practised specialist → 67, 69, 134

**second time around:** at the next try or attempt → 108, 111

**selective use:** targeted, purposeful, discerning, or careful usage → 84-85, 134

**self-esteem:** self-worth, sense of worth, pride in oneself, faith in oneself → 14, 17

**shipment:** delivery, consignment → 119, 121

**similar issues:** much the same problems, concerns, or difficulties → 57, 59, 134

**simple virtues:** straightforward merits, assets, or good qualities → 49, 52, 134

**simplified:** easier, simpler, streamlined, reduced to essentials → 41, 44, 134

**smooth handling:** efficient or well-organised processing → 124, 126

**sole:** only, single, one and only, solitary → 6, 8, 134

**something is abandoned:** something is stopped, given up, or dispensed with → 59, 134

**sought-after:** very popular, very much in demand → 100, 102, 134

**spare parts kit:** extra, additional, or reserve set of components → 82, 84, 134

**special request:** particular wish, demand, desire, or pleading → 35, 134

**state-of-the-art:** up to date, modern, advanced → 30

**steep:** high, expensive, costly → 6, 8, 134-135

**still need to be developed:** yet require to be tapped or opened up → 94-95, 135

**stinginess is cool:** thriftiness is in, parsimony is great → 69, 72, 135

**storage:** stockroom, storehouse, warehouse, depot → 15, 18, 32, 35, 135

**storage costs:** warehouse or stockroom expenses → 15, 18, 32

**strengths and weaknesses:** good and bad points, positive and negative sides → 104, 108, 111

**subconsciously:** unknowingly, unwittingly, inadvertently, unintentionally → 36, 38, 135

**subliminal:** unconscious, hidden, unintentional → 38-39, 135

**to announce:** to make known, to report, to disclose, to reveal → 125

**to appoint:** to designate, to nominate, to select, to choose, to settle on, to decide on → 66, 68, 135

**to appreciate someone:** to value, esteem, or think highly of someone → 54, 135

**to appreciate something greatly:** to be very thankful or grateful for something → 9, 135

**to arise from this:** to appear, surface, evolve, or emerge from this → 111

**to arise:** to surface, to develop, to crop up, to appear, to evolve → 25, 68, 102, 111, 135

**to arrange with someone to do something:** to make preparations or plans for someone to do something → 121

**to associate as peers:** to mix, keep company, or deal with each other as equals → 128, 135

**to attempt:** to try, to make an effort, to endeavour, to strive, to venture → 51, 135

**to attune to:** to adjust to, to adapt to, to familiarise oneself with → 66, 68, 135

**to be a native of:** to be a citizen or national of → 68, 135

**to be a no-no for someone:** to be a taboo, unmentionable, banned, or prohibited for someone → 22

**to be able to afford something:** to have the funds for, manage to pay for, or find the money for something → 16-17

**to be advantageous:** to be beneficial, helpful, useful, or of benefit → 88-9, 135-136

**to be agreeable towards:** to consent to, to accept, to approve of, to assent to → 9, 136

**to be angry about something:** to be annoyed, irritated, gnashing one's teeth, or furious about something → 121

**to be at risk:** to be in danger, in peril, or in jeopardy → 127, 136

**to be attuned to:** to be adjusted, tailored, fitted, or assimilated to → 88, 136

**to be bothersome:** to be troublesome, inconvenient, incommodious, or annoying → 56, 136

**to be bound to fail:** to most likely go under, be unsuccessful, or fall short → 79, 136

**to be cajoled into something:** to be wheedled or coaxed into something → 9-10, 136

**to be conducted:** to be carried out, performed, or done → 125

**to be convenient:** to be opportune, useful, or favourable → 111

**to be deprived of:** to be denied, to lack, to be deficient of, to be left without → 92, 136

**to be determined:** to be resolved, set, or intent → 12, 50, 110, 136

**to be disclosed to one:** to be revealed, divulged, or unveiled to one → 76, 136

**to be evasive:** to be hard to pin down, vague, equivocal, or indirect → 22, 136

**to be even more essential:** to be all the more important, crucial, or necessary → 44-45, 136

**to be exemplified by:** to be demonstrated, shown, or represented by → 63, 136

**to be faced with a challenge:** to be confronted with a difficult task → 114, 136

**to be genuinely interested:** to be truly or really intrigued → 86, 88

**to be greatly tempted:** to be very much at risk, provoked, or enticed → 51-52, 136

**to be in charge of something:** to be in command of, in control of, or responsible for something → 60, 112, 136

**to be in touch with something:** to be familiar with, no stranger to, or accustomed to something → 69, 136

**to be intangible:** to be impalpable or untouchable → 112

**to be less of a concern:** to be not as much a cause of worry or unease → 47, 136,

**to be maintained:** to be kept up, continued, kept going, or carried on → 88, 136,

**to be meliorated:** to be refined, fine-tuned, perfected, or honed → 64, 136

**to be more sensible:** to be more judicious, sagacious, prudent, perceptive, or farsighted → 68, 136

**to be obligated:** to be required, compelled, obliged, or duty-bound → 59, 136

**to be overly zealous:** to be too hasty, eager, keen, intense, or forceful → 29, 136

**to be perceived objectively:** to be seen neutrally or without bias or prejudice → 63-64, 136

**to be promising:** to show high potential → 76, 136

**to be prone to breaking down:** to be likely, disposed, or predisposed to stop working → 29, 136

**to be pure luck:** to be good fortune, a sheer blessing, or an utter stroke of luck → 88, 136-137

**to be quite varied:** to be very diverse, different, or unlike → 102, 137

**to be readily available:** to be promptly, quickly, or at once accessible → 60, 137

**to be responsible for something:** to be accountable for in charge of something → 57, 137

**to be retired:** to have given up work, to have stopped working, to be pensioned off → 102, 137

**to be so dumbfounded:** to be so flab-bergasted, astonished, astounded, taken aback, or stunned → 22, 137

**to be very determined:** to be enormously set, bent, or intent → 21, 137

**to be virtually ubiquitous:** to be practically ever-present or omnipresent → 25, 137

**to be well-suited for:** to be good, right, or well qualified for → 121

**to be wrested:** to be wrung, taken away, or removed → 95, 137

**to bear fruit:** to show results, to pay off, to be successful, to produce results → 72, 137

**to beat one to the punch:** to win the race, to be faster or quicker than oneself → 38, 137

**to become annoyed:** to become angry, irritated, exasperated, or upset → 114, 137

**to become apparent:** to become clear, evident, obvious, plain, discernible, or noticeable → 94, 120, 137

**to bemoan:** to complain, moan, or grumble about → 106, 137

**to bid farewell to something:** to be without or give up something → 39, 137

**to bless:** to provide, to bestow, to endow → 72

**to blossom:** to flourish, to thrive, to grow → 79, 137

**to campaign:** to work, to stand up, to fight, to champion → 80, 137

**to cater precisely to:** to meet, to fulfil, to comply with, to fit → 103, 137

**to climb the social ladder:** to get ahead, to get somewhere, to rise in the world → 61, 137

**to coerce:** to force, to pressure, to bully → 11

**to come across as pushy:** to be perceived as aggressive or forceful → 25, 137

**to come away empty-handed:** to miss out, to fail to benefit, to lose out → 21, 137

**to come to an interesting conclusion:** to learn of a compelling result or outcome → 30, 137

**to compare notes:** to exchange, share, or pass on information, to swap opinions → 72, 137

**to complete:** to finish off, to make perfect, to add the finishing or final touch to → 30, 58-59, 137

**to concern oneself with something:** to busy oneself with or devote one's time to something → 25, 137

**to consolidate:** to combine, to merge, to unite, to join, to fuse, to amalgamate → 43, 137

**to constrain:** to hinder, to restrict, to hamper, to limit → 39, 137

**to corner someone:** to trap someone, to pin someone down, to back someone into a corner → 9, 137

**to correlate:** to show a relationship, to draw a parallel, to equate, to associate → 35, 137-138

**to crave attention:** to long for, yearn for, or hunger after being noticed → 116, 138

**to cross the 50s threshold:** to turn 50, to celebrate one's 50th birthday → 50 102, 138

**to crumble:** to disintegrate, to fall to pieces, to deteriorate, to go down → 75, 138

**to curtail:** to limit, to reduce, to shorten → 79

**to cut down:** to reduce, to decrease → 59, 138

**to cut off:** to break off, to disconnect, to suspend, to discontinue, to intercept → 47, 138

**to decrease:** to diminish, to decline, to dwindle, to shrink, to fall, to lessen → 47, 59, 75, 79, 138

**to derive from:** to get, receive, acquire, obtain, or gain from → 10

**to desire:** to want, to wish for, to long for, to set one's heart on → 10

**to devalue:** to diminish, to detract from, to fail to recognise, to bring down → 55, 138

**to devote:** to assign, to allot, to set aside, to offer, to dedicate → 110

**to dig deep into one's pockets:** to spend a lot of money → 102, 138

**to discontinue:** to stop, to come to a halt, to be terminated or broken off → 47, 111

**to display extra caution:** to show evidence of added carefulness, attention, heed, watchfulness, or concern → 68, 138

**to dispose of something:** to get rid of something, to clear something out, to leave something behind → 40, 72, 138

**to disregard:** to ignore, to forget about, to overlook, to turn a blind eye to → 11, 138

**to distinguish oneself from:** to set oneself apart from, to separate oneself from → 48, 64, 89, 138

**to distinguish oneself from someone:** to differentiate oneself from someone → 48, 138

**to draw one's conclusions:** to come to a deduction, assumption, presumption, or inference → 22, 138

**to drop everything:** to leave or abandon your work → 116, 138

**to elucidate:** to explain, to make clear, to clarify, to reveal → 7, 9, 103, 138

**to embark on:** to set out on, to tackle, to enter on, to take up, to engage in → 59, 138

**to embrace:** to accept, to adopt → 62, 64, 138

**to enable:** to allow, to entitle, to empower, to make it possible for, to permit → 48, 72

**to enter into:** to record in, to put in, to write in, to document in → 58, 60, 138

**to enter unknown territory:** to go into an unfamiliar or unexplored area → 97, 138

**to entertain considerable doubt:** to harbour scepticism, uneasiness, apprehension, or distrust → 29, 138

**to equip:** to provide, to furnish, to supply, to endow → 44, 138

**to evade:** to avoid, to dodge, to shake off, to sidestep → 108, 111

**to expect a great deal:** to make great demands, to be more demanding → 102, 138

**to experience defeat:** to encounter setback or disappointment → 52, 138

**to experience such a hassle:** to go through, suffer, or encounter such difficulties → 121

**to fear:** to be afraid of, to worry about, to be anxious about, to be scared of, to dread → 10-11, 84, 138

**to feed someone's hopes:** to make empty promises to someone → 25, 138

**to feel more obligated:** to feel more compelled, obliged, or duty-bound → 25-26, 138

**to feel uneasy:** to feel tense, ill at ease, anxious, apprehensive, uncomfortable, or edgy → 8, 22, 138

**to fetch:** to sell for, to go for, to bring in, to yield → 17

**to figure something out:** to understand or comprehend something → 12, 138

**to firmly root:** to securely anchor, to strongly embed → 42, 45, 138

**to flatter:** to butter up, to soft-soap, to play up to → 18

**to gain traction on:** to establish oneself on, to gain access to the market on, to break into the market on → 67-69, 138

**to get the bid:** to win the contract → 25, 138

**to give someone similarly high marks:** to give someone likewise excellent grades or scores → 64, 138-139

**to go into something:** to tackle, deal with, or apply oneself to something → 26, 139

**to go without saying:** to be a given, to be a normal thing, to be completely natural → 22, 139

**to greatly amplify:** to significantly increase, augment, boost, or magnify → 57, 59, 139

**to hail from:** to come from, to be a native of, to be born in, to have one's roots in → 68, 139

**to hang on:** to hold out, to stay close → 24, 26, 139

**to hardly differ:** to barely be different or dissimilar → 97, 139

**to haul in:** to pull in, to bring in, to rake in, to generate → 48, 139

**to have a knack for something:** to have a skill, talent, flair, or a special ability for something → 102, 139

**to have at one's disposal:** to have available or on hand → 91, 139

**to have come up with:** to have created, thought up, originated, or conceived → 72, 139

**to have failed:** to have been unsuccessful, fallen through, or not succeeded → 110-111

**to have good taste:** to have style, elegance, stylishness, or finesse → 82, 84, 139

**to have one's work cut out for oneself:** to have a big task or undertaking ahead of oneself → 126

**to have opened up all possibilities:** to have taken advantage of or utilised all options → 127, 139

**to have to grapple with something:** to have to struggle with, come to grips with, or deal with something → 72, 139

**to heat up:** to boost, to increase, to expand, to develop, to amplify → 97

**to help oneself to:** to take, to take possession of, to walk off with → 36, 139

**to hijack:** to take over, to take control of, to seize → 38, 139

**to hurt no one:** to upset, cause sorrow to, or cause anguish to nobody → 39, 139

**to illustrate:** to exemplify, to demonstrate, to show → 34-5, 139

**to indicate:** to be a sign, to signify, to show, to reveal, to imply → 10

**to induce someone to do something:** to cause, get, or prompt someone to do something → 18

**to inspect:** to take a close look at, to examine, to check out → 40, 96, 98, 139

**to intently concern oneself with:** to be very interested in or involved with → 21-22, 139

**to inundate:** to overwhelm, to swamp, to overburden, to bog down → 29, 139

**to issue:** to hand out, to distribute, to give out, to release, to circulate → 139

**to jam:** to obstruct, to block, to clog, to congest, to clice off → 39, 139

**to keep cropping up:** to continue to happen, to get in the way, to occur, to turn up → 52, 139

**to keep in mind:** to remember, to not forget, to take into consideration → 16

**to keep something in check:** to keep something within bounds, to not go overboard with something → 125-126

**to label as:** to consider, regard, classify, characterise, or designate as → 35, 139

**to lack the motivation:** to not have, be deficient in, or be short of the enthusiasm → 52, 139

**to leave tacitly:** to go away quietly, to depart without saying a word → 111

**to let oneself in for something:** to get involved or caught up in something → 25, 139

**to level the price down:** to beat down, knock down, or cut the cost → 9, 139

**to link:** to connect, to bring together → 44, 139

**to make a face:** to grimace, to frown, to have a distorted expression, to scowl → 22, 139

**to make one aware of something:** to make one conscious of or open one's eyes to something → 16

**to make someone suspicious:** to cause someone to become doubtful, unsure, sceptical, wary, or leery → 8, 139

**to make up one's mind to do something:** to come to a decision or reach a conclusion to do something → 29, 139

**to no longer be content:** to not be satisfied or comfortable any longer → 11, 139

**to not be a constant:** to not be a steady factor, an absolute term, or an invariable → 83, 140

**to not be able to pull the wool over someone's eyes:** to not be able to fool, trick, deceive, or dupe someone → 73

**to not be adding value:** to not be increasing or augmenting worth → 44, 140

**to not be afraid of something:** to not be fearful of or nervous about something → 8, 140

**to not be aware of something:** to not be conscious or in the know about something → 88, 140

**to not be completely done in:** to not be utterly exhausted, worn out, tired out, beat, or fatigued → 61, 140

**to not be content:** to not be satisfied, pleased, or comfortable → 114, 140

**to not be perceived as:** to not be understood, identified, or regarded as → 125

**to not be willing:** to not be prepared, ready, keen, agreeable, or disposed → 34, 140

**to not comply with:** to not fulfil, follow, obey, conform to, or adhere to → 83, 140

**to not lapse into:** to not slide, slip, submerge, or drift into → 8, 140

**to not let oneself be put off:** to not let oneself be turned away or brushed off → 25, 140

**to not stand out:** to not attrack attention or catch the eye → 38, 140

**to open up:** to develop, to build up → 70, 72, 76, 140

**to open up new vistas:** to result in a new perspective or outlook → 76

**to outweigh:** to be more important than, to take precedence over → 9, 140

**to overcome:** to conquer, to surmount, to rise above, to prevail over → 46, 48, 140

**to pass the time:** to while away, occupy, or spend the hours → 114-115, 140

**to pave the way for something:** to prepare, clear the way, or make preparations for something → 88, 140

**to place emphasis on:** to put importance, attention, weight, or accent on → 126

**to preclude:** to prevent, to prohibit, to make impossible, to rule out, to bar → 84, 140

**to preferentially assign:** to make a point of allocating, allotting, giving, or apportioning → 68, 140

**to procrastinate:** to postpone or delay action, to move action to the back burner → 52, 56, 140

**to procrastinate in doing something:** to put off, delay, postpone, or adjourn doing something → 56, 140

**to propose:** to offer, to suggest → 79, 140

**to prove to be:** to turn out to be, to end up being, to emerge as, to become → 98, 140

**to push through:** to get through, to get accepted → 95, 140

**to put on the back burner:** to put on ice, to postpone, to defer, to put off → 59-60, 140

**to put someone in their place:** to humble someone, to take someone down a peg or two → 72, 140-141

**to put someone off:** to discourage, dissuade, dishearten, or repel someone → 12, 141

**to quadruple:** to multiply by four → 35, 141

**to recapture:** to bring back, to return with, to go and get, to get hold of, to win back, to regain, to recover, to reclaim → 52, 107, 110, 141

**to recruit:** to hire, to sign up, to take on, to enlist, to enrol → 45, 141

**to refrain from:** to do without, to hold back, to forgo, to avoid → 83, 98, 141, 155

**to remain unresponsive to something:** to stay indifferent or impassive to something → 11

**to render:** to provide, to give, to deliver, to supply, to make available → 88, 141

**to replace:** to take the place of, to supersede, to succeed, to come after → 30, 97, 141

**to rescue someone from:** to save someone from, to get → 116, 141

**to resume:** to start again, to recommence, to restart, to take up again → 107, 111

**to reward oneself for something:** to give oneself a present for something → 17

**to ring hollow:** to not seem credible, authentic, genuine, or convincing → 9, 141

**to run into a lot of money:** to be quite expensive or costly → 30, 141

**to safely assume something:** to take something for granted, to surely expect something → 89, 141

**to seek advice from:** to consult with → 26, 141

**to seem suspicious:** to appear to be dubious, to give the impression of being suspect → 22, 141

**to show consideration for someone:** to display thoughtfulness or respect for someone → 125

**to shrink:** to get smaller, to reduce, to drop off, to shrivel → 47, 75, 141

**to sink deep into one's memory:** to learn by heart, to commit to one's memory → 10, 141

**to stay true to someone:** to remain loyal, faithful, or dedicated to someone → 79, 141

**to stem from something:** to arise from, originate from, be rooted in, or derive from something → 68

**to stick to one's guns:** to remain firm, resolute, determined, or unwavering → 25, 141

**to stick to one's set objectives:** to adhere to one's determined goals or targets → 52, 141

**to substantiate:** to give substance to, to demonstrate, to corroborate → 63, 141

**to substitute for:** to replace with, to exchange for, to use instead of, to switch with → 30, 141

**to take a liking to something:** to take pleasure in or enjoy something → 17

**to take a new run at it:** to try again, to have another go at it → 24, 26, 141

**to take one's time:** to proceed → 30, 141

**to take precedence:** to come first, to take priority, to be considered most critical → 9, 51

**to tap:** to draw on, to use, to make use of, to utilise, to put to use, to exhaust, to exploit → 68, 127, 141

**to tend to be more apt:** to have a propensity to be true, correct, on target, or exactly right → 126

**to terminate:** to end, to stop → 111

**to throw someone a curve:** to take someone unawares, to throw someone off their guard → 112

**to tune out:** to turn away from it all, to stop paying attention → 85, 141

**to unburden:** to relieve, to soothe, to ease, to alleviate, to mitigate, to assuage → 61, 141

**to undercut:** to undersell, to beat, to charge less than, to underbid, to best → 47, 141

**to utter:** to say, to speak, to express, to voice, to state → 29, 141

**to valorise:** to enhance, to improve, to boost, to enrich, to reinforce → 55, 141

**to revert to something:** to fall back on, resort to, or make use of something → 120

**to ward off:** to fend off, to beat off, to stave off, to avert, to rule out, to repel, to repulse, to keep at bay, to fight off → 38, 45, 47, 107, 111, 141

**to weave:** to create, to put together, to contrive, to make up, to fabricate → 66, 68, 141

**to withdraw something:** to take something back, to retract something → 111

**trade fair:** exhibition, exposition, show → 125

**tremendous:** great, enormous, immense → 97-98, 141

**truth dawned on him:** reality struck or occurred to him → 10-11, 141

**unfolding:** developing, progressing, evolving → 119, 121

**unique:** only one of its kind, exceptional, inimitable, without equal, unmatched → 46, 54, 141-142

**unknown entity:** unfamiliar organisation or film → 37, 39, 142

**used-up:** not being able to make use of again, old → 69-72, 142

**utmost:** greatest, highest, maximum → 46, 48, 57, 59, 142

**variant:** variation, modification, option, alternative → 32-34, 121, 142

**variation:** version, alternative, variant, adaptation → 34, 119, 121

**various sources:** a variety of, a range of, different, assorted, or mixed origins → 41, 44, 142

**victim:** an easy prey or target, a drupe → 36, 38, 142

**was commissioned:** was authorised, empowered, or accredited → 67, 69, 142

**wastage:** deviation from spreading or distribution → 90, 92, 142

**we sincerely apologise:** we genuinely ask for forgiveness, we express our heartfelt regret → 118, 121

**wear and tear:** signs of use, friction, deterioration, damage, or erosion → 14, 17

**were to be taken into account:** were to be considered, included, regarded, or taken into consideration → 90, 92, 142

**what do I get out of it:** how do I profit or benefit from it → 10-11, 142

**when in doubt:** when undecided, uncertain, unsure, or doubtful → 9

**wholesale:** in bulk, in large quantities → 41, 44, 142

**will be carried out:** will be done, completed, accomplished, implemented, or executed → 117, 120

**with great dismay:** with utter consternation, with deep regret, with great concern → 118, 121

**words of salutation:** getting or welcome phrases → 53-54, 142

**worst case scenario:** most terrible, awful, or unpleasant future situation → 15, 18

**you are entitled to it:** you are worthy of or qualified for it → 18

**you deserve it:** you earn it, you have a right to have it → 16, 18

**MANAGEMENT**

**INFORMÁTICA**

**CULTURA GENERAL**

## RELACIONES

## ESPIRITUALIDAD

## SALUD